TRADE-OFF

TRADE OFF

OFF
BY
Alfy Smith

Trade-Off

The events and conversations in this book are based upon the author's memories of them and any unwitting errors that may appear on its pages are the author's own. Song lyrics have been used with permission from their creators.

Editor: Deborah Froese
Cover and Interior Design: Emma Elzinga
Cover Photo: Stephanie Phillps

Indigo River Publishing
3 West Garden Street, Ste. 718
Pensacola, FL 32502
www.indigoriverpublishing.com

Ordering Information:
Quantity sales: Special discounts are available on quantity purchases by corporations, associations, and others. For details, contact the publisher at the address above.
Orders by US trade bookstores and wholesalers: Please contact the publisher at the address above.

Library of Congress Control Number: 2022938789
ISBN: 978-1-954676-32-9 (paperback) 978-1-954676-33-6 (ebook)

First Edition

With Indigo River Publishing, you can always expect great books, strong voices, and meaningful messages. Most importantly, you'll always find . . . words worth reading.

To the loving memory of my mother,

Ms. Elizabeth Williams;

my baby brother, Vonsha J. Blow;

and my beloved wife, Felicia Katrice Johnson–Smith.

Introduction

WHAT DO YOU want out of life? Think about your biggest desires and dreams. What do you seek? Then be assured that whatever you want will come at a cost, even many costs. Those costs you pay are the trade-offs you must make.

Some trade-offs are easy, and some are painful. Some you make willingly, and some are forced. But as sure as you have to pay for your groceries before you leave the store with them, you must make trade-offs in life to get its greatest rewards.

One price you must surely pay is dedication to your path: that pure commitment to a task or purpose, that singular focus, that eye on the prize. A lot of us know it, but do we live it? You likely know how difficult that struggle can be.

Even though we hear words like dedication, persistence, and grit from the time we're young, it's a sad fact that not everyone lives up to their full potential. Many are only dedicated to a point. Once they reach that point, their commitment drops off. The trade-off is not paid, and the reward is lost.

The good things in life only come if you make the right trade-offs. The price—the trade-off—must be paid: life for death, honor for dishonor, wealth for poverty, and strength for weakness. Trade-offs even lead to embodying and accepting that which you once were not.

Yes, many don't see their full potential, but I believe I did. I pushed when rock-like challenges wouldn't give, and I fought when it seemed there was nothing left worth fighting for.

I came to my trade-offs through the prism of something some people might view as trivial. But if I told you I was excelling in a business that generates billions of dollars worldwide, you might not think it so trivial. If I told you I worked in a field that brought hope to young Black kids and helped raise some out of the ghettos, who then shared their wealth to start schools, community programs, and scholarships, you might recognize its greatness. If you consider that it has now ascended from an American concern to an international passion in the villages of China, the cities of Greece, the playgrounds of Ecuador, and schoolyards in Spain, it wouldn't seem so trivial. I'm talking about the sport, the passion, and the art of . . . basketball.

Who am I? While I believe that Michael Jordan is the greatest of all time on the basketball court, I not only believe but had the chance to tell him in person that I could have easily defeated him in a pure shoot-out contest. (Mike, being the true competitor he is, had a laugh and recognized a kindred spirit.)

This isn't just self-proclaimed success; I have had folks tell me more than once that I was the greatest scorer of the basketball they had ever personally seen. Yet, in an instant, a devastating incident kept me out of the NBA. Still, my gift was not to be wasted.

My abilities brought me to the attention of one Roy Jones, Jr., the legendary boxer and my dear friend. Our lives merged, gifts were exchanged, and talents shared. Although my NBA career never materialized, God allowed me to experience the lifestyle of an NBA player through a different prism: the boxing ring, the trade-off you see on the cover of this book.

Roy was my gateway to a life that reached far beyond normal expectations. He valued me enough to bring me onto his team. He saw something in me that would elevate him as well. I can only smile humbly to think that I shared in the greater portion of his illustrious career.

Join me on a journey to discover what a lifestyle of supreme dedication can do for you.

But it comes with a price. Do you have what it takes?

I am Alfy Smith. Through my story, I hope to show you that when you take your gifts, your talents—everything that makes you special—you can find connections leading to a life that gives you something more than average. This is about the trade-offs we make and how we make them. I made some that paid off, and some that didn't. There are some that I'm still waiting to see pay off.

But please, take a little time with me. Let me show you the power and the pain, the time and the tears, the will and the way of making the trade-off because the trade-off leads to the payoff.

1. Where It All Started

I SAT STONE-LIKE in the crowded cell, my head down. I was determined that my eyes were not gonna get wet. I shifted between a searing heat pouring through my body, every hair at attention, and slumping into a hollow shell. Like a broken record, my mind kept pestering me with the question, how did I end up here? Every dream and aspiration I had, everything that Momma wanted—that all my supporters wanted—could not have been leading up to this.

My muscles tensed again, bracing with energy this time. I lifted my eyes, and the gray dingy walls fell out of focus as I saw the faces of those around me. None of these people wanted to be here any more than I did, and that included everyone outside of my cell doing thankless jobs. Mostly, they had faces frozen like weather-worn statues.

The situation just wasn't me. Life means more than just a circumstance. I could exchange all the callousness and negativity of my situation for something else. My head lifted a little more, and I began to smile.

I had a modest upbringing in Pensacola, Florida, USA. Say "Florida," and you conjure up visions of Paradise. The orange, glowing sun invigorates youthful bodies while sweet breezes give overworked souls a chance for rest. It's a real blessing to have daily access to those treasures. Pensacola is a relatively small city in the panhandle of Florida. The sugary white beaches and crystal-clear blue ocean are nothing short of breathtaking. At the same time, travel inland less than an hour in any direction, and you'll find the traditional features of the American South; thick woods with tall trees that are teeming with wildlife and muggy swamps.

Real-world reality and struggle have no boundaries. Behind the postcard-perfect scenes sit the ugly difficulties of life. Like most folks, I wasn't immune to struggle as a boy, but I did have a truly happy childhood.

Years before, my granddaddy on my momma's side, Ulysses Williams, came to Florida from Eufaula, Alabama with one hundred dollars and a third-grade education. Like a lot of Black folks back then, he was determined to make the best life he could for his future family. He worked tirelessly to become a master carpenter and eventually rose to the thirty-third degree with the Freemasons. He started a family. Fast-forward to April 16, 1966, and I came into the world by means of his daughter, Susie Elizabeth Williams.

I was born right at the boiling point of the civil rights era. By the time I went to school, I was already living with the benefits of that powerful shift in our country. Pensacola schools began to desegregate early in 1962. I went to school with a good mix of kids, and I've been blessed to grow up with an unprejudiced view of people. I really don't care what color you are; you are my brother or sister as long as you're trying to do right.

My father proved to be a big-hearted man. You could really say big hearts run in my family. His pride in me was always clear. When we went to church, he always made sure I had the sharpest hats, just like him. That must have made some kind of an impression on me because to this day, if you ask anyone who knows me, I never leave the house without a sharp hat or a fresh cap. (Man, every color of Kangol cap they made, I got it!)

Naturally, I was a little spoiled. Being finicky at meals usually meant a scolding or a whooping for most poor kids. I never had that worry. For whatever reason, I couldn't get enough bread, and my family would trip over that. I used to just grab a loaf of bread and start munching on it as my whole lunch meal.

Momma would stare at me like I had grown another head. "Boy, what are you doing?"

I'd keep smacking away, smirking and oblivious.

Daddy would just let me be. "If he wanna eat the bread, let him eat the bread!" He'd chuckle and wave Momma off.

Even when he would take me out for hot dogs, I'd grab the dog with my little nubby fingers, toss it away, and dig into the bun. Daddy would laugh and smile.

I loved that smile.

Life flipped inside out when I reached the age of five. That year, Daddy was cut down in his prime by cancer. He was quite a bit older than Momma but was still much too young to go that soon. I never grasped all that was going on around me in the days following. Everything was gray and still.

That stillness was a truly awkward sensation because the days leading up to Daddy's funeral were full of activity. People shuffled around like they were afraid to wake someone up. Then without warning, a sharp howl of grief would puncture the quiet. There were days of grief, the funeral, and then nothing. Everyone was gone. For a while, there was nothing but a big hole, a hole in the house, a hole in Momma's heart, and a hole I too felt but couldn't fully comprehend. Young and determined, Momma braced herself and set to working hard taking care of me.

At that point, I was Momma's only child with half brothers and sisters from my daddy that I didn't get to know too well while growing up. But the hole left by Daddy was like a vacuum that other family members quickly rushed in to fill. And family would come in unique ways from unique places.

Romances come and go in life, and they can leave a rocky road of regret and heartache. A lot of people get bitter and resentful. But I learned a powerful lesson about moving away from that bitterness. After my daddy's death, his first wife and my momma became best friends. When I tell you they became best friends, I'm not telling you any stories. Those were two women who did anything and everything together until the end. The night Momma died, well, they had just been on a trip to Louisiana together that day.

I grew up knowing my daddy's first wife as "Aunt Bet-

ty." I didn't understand the true nature of their relationship. After I got old enough to understand, seeing the
power of love that she and Momma both lived out only
made me love her more. I then began to affectionately
call her "Stepmomma."

Their history never became an issue or a cause for
tension. The way they didn't let pettiness come between
them taught me a valuable lesson: there is no need to
fight or be bitter in life. Treat people good, and you'll get
good right back. Trade being bitter for being better.

Big hearts were a part of Stepmomma's blood too,
which must have been why she and Momma were so
close. After my daddy died, Stepmomma was out riding with her dad. They got to talking about my daddy,
and he said plainly, "You know, she [Momma] is gonna
need some help." Just like that, they stepped in to support Momma. It soothes me now thinking of all these
big hearts and love that I'm surrounded by.

I'm proud to say that I've done my best to live up to
that. I don't hang on to anger or resentment. Mr. Dean
Pendleton, with whom I worked at Ruby Gainer Charter
School, used to tell people, "If you can't get along with
Smitty [me], then something is wrong with you." That
attitude has allowed me to build strong relationships all

ALFY SMITH | 7

my life.

Momma constantly imparted to me the value of honesty, and I did my best to never let her down. One day, Momma was across the street at a neighbor lady's house. Me and my good friend Pookie (my longtime friend, Sherman Foster) wanted to run and get a snack from the Charlie Chips corner store. We sprinted across the street to find Momma.

"Momma," I begged, "can I have two dollars to go to Charlie Chips for a snack?"

"Sure, baby," she said. "Go ahead."

I went to her purse to get the two dollars. Momma's neighbor friend cut her eyes in disbelief. "You let him go in your purse like that?"

"Alfy ain't gonna take anything out more than what he asked for," Momma explained. She trusted me like that because that was how she trained me.

She would tell me about things that went on when she cleaned houses. She would notice that people might leave something out, like a ring or some money. It was a sort of test. These were items that they could afford to lose, but valuable enough that they would notice them gone. If something came up missing, then they knew you couldn't be trusted. Momma never took a thing that didn't belong to her. She wasn't tempted to take advantage of anyone, even if it might seem they could afford to lose it.

I got the point. Treat people right, and they'll do right by you.

My Granddaddy Ulysses stepped up to the plate in a big way after my daddy was gone. He now became "Daddy" to me and was the only daddy I ever really knew. He was a rock of wisdom and guidance. He would call Momma almost every night, his deep, rolling voice pouring out the phone. "Hey, boy, let me speak to Black Meat," he'd say.

Momma would grab the phone in a tone of mock annoyance. "Man, what you want?!"

Then they'd giggle and chat, sometimes for hours. That respect and love were impressed upon me. From very young, I picked up the habit of calling my grandmomma weekly and sometimes talking for hours with her.

Yes, you can trade off a lot of things in life, but a loving family is not something to ever let go of.

Grandmomma and I gained an unshakable bond. I would stay with her and Daddy Ulysses during summers when I was very young. Wherever she fell asleep on the couch or in an easy chair, I would lay right there, curled up like a puppy, and sleep at her feet. She taught me so much. Since I had to be in the house on my own a lot when Momma was out working, I often called Grandmomma on the phone. She taught me how to prepare meals for myself and take care of anything I was worried about.

Since she tended to favor me, the other grandkids learned to use it to their advantage. They made sure I went along with her on her trips to the store. Grandmomma always wanted to get the Corn Flakes cereal with the rooster on the box. (We kids didn't want that stuff!) But if I was with her, she would get the cereal I wanted. I was really blessed with some wonderful relationships. I know not everyone is so fortunate.

In 1969, a few years after my birth, a pivotal figure was born, pivotal not just in my life, but on the world scene: Roy Levesta Jones, Jr. He too hails from Pensacola, Florida. Pound for pound, Roy Jones, Jr. is considered one of the top twenty boxers in history.

Roy—or RJJ, as he's sometimes known—was raised by a father who had been a boxer and was tougher than old shoe leather. He wanted to form his son in his image, for better or worse. I can't take anything away from what he gave to Roy in his training. It led Roy to be an all-time great. But Roy would need other figures to fashion himself into a complete athlete and man.

In some ways, Roy's life and mine are completely parallel: a love of sports, recognition of gifts in our respective crafts at a young age, a drive to win at almost any cost. But we also could be a study in opposites. I lost my daddy young and relied on a string of influential mentors to get me through. I never seemed to lack having a warm, solid, God-fearing man in my life to point me in the right direction.

On the other hand, Roy's relationship with his father—Big Roy—was complicated, a pressure cooker that always demanded the best of Roy. He was taught to be fierce, to trust few, and to show ruthless determination. This may seem cold and heartless, but one can never deny that the guidance Roy received paid off in grand ways. Big Roy cared about his son in his own way. Roy embraced his gifts and training and rode them to the pinnacle of greatness.

One day, we would have reason to meet, but it took some years before we got there. It would lead to one of my biggest and most valuable trade-offs. What was the key to this happening? Let me tell you about my special gift.

2. Newness

THE BEAUTY OF family in my growing up years was that we all took care of each other. It was nothing for me to go stay with an auntie for the weekend or even over a whole summer. I had cousins who would come stay with us without a second thought. Never mind that none of us had more than two nickels to rub together. Instead of looking at a new arrival as one more mouth to feed, the adults just took us in as a blessing.

Some of my best memories were with my cousin, David. I stayed with him during some summers once I got a little older. One night we were up watching the old gridiron football comedy, *The Longest Yard*, giggling and snickering without any consideration for sleeping adults. A scene came on where one player hit another in the groin. Well, you know that's hilarious for two little boys. Auntie came in and threatened us with a whooping if we cut up again.

Of course, not a few minutes later, a scene came up where someone got hit in the groin again. David couldn't contain himself. He bust out laughing and ran away down the hall, leaving me in the TV room to be caught and whooped by Auntie. We can look back and laugh about it now, but I wanted to get him for that!

Being poor was no obstacle to us enjoying what we did have. I didn't have any action figure toys to play with, so I would sit on the floor with two tennis shoes and make them wrestle, which gave the adults a good chuckle. Then on Saturdays, once everything was cleaned up and chores were done, Uncle Marvin and I would go down to the local TV station to watch the high-flying wrestlers. We learned a few dangerous moves, but thank goodness, no one got seriously hurt. I filled my passion for sports entertainment however I could.

All of this family association was back in a time before twenty-four-hour TV, video games, and internet. That meant that there was one thing to do, and that was to go outside and get on a field or a court. Basketball especially was something the bigger kids always seemed to be doing.

Something about the game resonated inside of me.

The first game I remember seeing on TV featured the world-famous Harlem Globetrotters. If you have never seen the Globetrotters play, do yourself a favor and first chance you get, watch one of their games. Legends like Curly Neal and Meadowlark Lemon were magicians with the ball. I sat in front of the screen, eyes fixated, locked in with sheer amazement.

Wow! The things they could do with the basketball. There was wizardry in their passing. A hand would fake left, but the ball went right. They displayed nearly impossible shooting, scooping from half court to *swish* through the basket. That's not even to mention the acrobatic dunks! It was all simply wondrous to me.

Who knows? Could this have been the moment when God endowed some special gifting or ability upon me? All I know is those Globetrotters in their star-spangled red, white, and blue uniforms sparked something in my heart that tingled with excitement.

One warm sunny day when I was eight years old, my teen-aged uncles and their friends were on a dirt court playing the usual game of twenty-one, a classic basketball game of every man for himself. I sat watching on the porch, a little boy in admiration of the older kids. I couldn't deny an itching to be out there. Of course, they would never invite me into a game, so I went over to ask to play, drawn to the joy and beauty of the sport.

"No, you too little. Go on, Alfy. Go on." They shooed me away. According to them, I'd get stomped on or knocked out in a heartbeat.

It wasn't enough to discourage me. I stayed on the sidelines gazing upon the action. The ball came loose on a wild rebound and rolled out of bounds to my feet. My uncle stood there waiting for me to pass him the ball. I picked it up and wrapped my hands around the warm rubber. Keep in mind, up until this point, I had never attempted to shoot a basketball. Getting the ball ten feet in the air to the hoop was like trying to summit Everest for a runty eight year old.

A warm rush gushed through me. I wasn't even thinking. I just did what came naturally, what I'd seen done a hundred times before. I skipped and hopped, triple-dribbling the ball. Then I clumsily picked it up with two hands and let it rip with everything I had.

The ball soared what felt like fifty feet in the air from my tiny viewpoint. Everyone's heads turned towards the basket. Like a slow-motion movie scene, the ball sailed through the air until it made that beautiful sound: swish!

"Ooooh!"

All the neighborhood boys started going crazy! You would have thought that I was a Globetrotter. My little friends who were watching started oohing and aahing too. Everyone went wild over that one shot.

Was it a premonition of things to come?

My Uncle Clint (everyone says I look like him) couldn't believe it. He called out, "Give it to him again!"

The ball was tossed back my way, and I again clumsily skipped, hopped, triple dribbled, and gave it all I had. Up, up, up it glided and . . .

Swish!

Everyone broke out in more cheers. "Ooooh!"

"Go on, Alfy!"

"Woo! Kid can ball!"

I stood there in disbelief myself, too stunned to really bask in the glow of the congratulations. Then the ball came right back to me.

"Shoot it, Alfy!"

I make the same childlike steps, gave the same Herculean effort, and got the same beautiful swish!

The court erupted again.

"Ooooh!"

"You know he did it! You know he did it!"

"That's what I'm talking about!"

The ball landed back in my hands, and I was feeling it. I let it rip again. It sailed high enough, floating beautifully. It looked like it was good and . . .

Ping!

It was off just by a bit, hitting the back of the rim and bouncing out.

"Aw," the boys moaned.

"Oh well. Still, that boy can shoot."

As the teens went back to their game, I received a few more pats on the back and words of encouragement. A lot of them stared at me like I was some kind of alien or something. I can only imagine that they wished they had whatever I had. I was overwhelmed with pride in my achievement. Hey, I started my career as a seventy-five percent shooter! How many can say that? That last miss had done nothing to diminish my elation.

So that's how the legend began.

I'm glad to say that, unlike some young men, I have never suffered from the disease of addiction to drugs or drinking. Some say the high from that first hit of drugs can sweep you up into a dreamlike state where you're always chasing it again and again. Well, the sensation of making those shots—my first three shots ever—became my drug of choice. That's a fulfilling high, a healthy high.

I encourage young people to stay away from the dangers of drugs and alcohol abuse. Find what can give you a natural high, what you can pour yourself into and get real joy, not something artificial.

The feeling of achievement was outstanding. Once I got home, I couldn't wait to share my joy with Momma. When I did, she beamed and fawned over me. What a day!

From that experience, I internalized another lesson. For any kids, whether your own kids, young relatives, or children in your neighborhood and community, be their biggest cheerleader. Help them to seize their dreams and to embrace whatever it is that makes them special. While I had gifts that would give me a celebrated name in my hometown and lead to some great things, I've never shied from tooting the horn of young ones coming up who show remarkable skill, whether on the court, in music, on the field, or in the ring. There's no jealousy. When we support each other, we get greater as a people.

But was my early aptitude just a fluke, just some kind of beginner's luck?

3. Oh Yeah, It Feels So Good

THERE WAS NO time to stick around and bask in my little bit of newfound fame. The following week, Momma shipped me off to spend the summer with her twin sisters, Minnie and Mary Williams, in Dallas, Texas. Just like all my family, they didn't complain about another mouth to feed. They took me in as one of their own.

It was a typical, fun-filled summer, and before I knew it, it was time to go back home. I was put on a plane by myself as an eight-year-old boy. It's hard to believe there was a time when you could do such a thing. I love the good things the modern world has brought us, but I miss the time when you could trust your neighbor like that. I've gotta give much love to the flight attendants who took good care of me that day.

My Auntie Marcella Williams and Charles Willoughby, her boyfriend, were there to pick me up when I arrived home. They warmly greeted me. And we headed on our way to Grandmomma's.

But first, we stopped at the mall. That surprised me. Why are we going here? I wondered. We made our way inside and went to the shoe store.

"Come on, Alfy," they said. "Let's check to see what size you are."

My heart started pumping a little faster. They're not really going to . . .

No.

Yes!

They got me a pair of Brand. New. Black. Converse. Chuck. Taylors. All Stars. I knew I was a bad man now! I was practically floating when we left the mall. Those were the shoes the pros wore, even the Globetrotters. I couldn't wait to test them out. (Let me tell you, before the Currys and Brons and even before Jordans, there was one true basketball shoe, and that was a pair of Chuck Taylors.)

After a quick stop at Granny's, I made my way to the Salvation Army Community Center gym. My buddy Paul King, who was a little older than me, immediately called out.

"Alfy over here!" Paul turned to Coach Chuck, who

led the kids my age. "Hey, you need to let my little home-boy play. That boy can shoot."

Some people may have had their reservations. I didn't exactly look the part yet. I had on my smooth black Chuck Taylors . . . with brown and yellow church socks. I'm surprised they didn't laugh me out of the gym, but Coach obliged. Now the stage was set for my true coming-out party.

That youth league was in its fourth game of the season. The boys had already made hooping a regular part of life. I was a pure novice. I hadn't done any kind of training camps or lessons. It was going to be just raw talent—as raw as raw can get.

I checked into the game, and man, I was like a fish in water. I'd get the ball and just like that first time a few months before, with no warmup, no nothing, swish. Swish. Swish. I was cooking.

In basketball nowadays, when a player's got it going, they say, "let him eat!" In other words, give him the ball and get out of the way! Well, they let me eat that day. It was a buffet!

That was the fourth game of their season. Four boys in the youth league were battling for leading scorer as well as the eventual Most Valuable Player (MVP) Award.

I wouldn't have been considered much of a threat just coming in. Yet, when the final buzzer rang, I was sitting on forty-eight points. After my performance in that one game, I became the leading scorer of the league. By the end of our season, I was also named MVP. I made a lot of new friends right then and surely some enemies as well. Either way, on the court, I was a wonder kid.

That's where another trade-off would come into play. I would now have a target on my back. Whether it was opponents or teammates, someone was bound to be jealous of my ability. At the time, I was just having fun. Thanks to the warm background I was raised in, I only focused on having fun with my friends on the court. Petty rivalries did not get in my way.

It may seem like a small thing but remember to have fun. Don't let the haters stop you from excelling in what you do best. So many people have missed opportunities in life for fear of what might happen to them. I could have been afraid to play or to miss a shot, but the encouragement I got was enough to carry me on.

That was just the start of my sports journey. More accolades and great things were on the way.

4. Feelin' It

I WAS JUST a natural when it came to sports. I can only call my ability God-given because I just had an eye for what needed to be done and a sixth sense for where to run, shoot, or throw. I was a rookie, but who knew? Kind of like Forrest Gump, you could put a ball in my hand, give instructions, and I could make it happen.

That comparison is fitting for so much of my life. I'm certainly not what you would call mentally slow, really just an average Joe when it came to school, but like the main character in that movie, my gifts opened up doors I could have never imagined outside of my wildest dreams, intersecting with monumental figures in sports, business, and government.

My love for basketball grew day by day. Our season ended way too soon for me. But just as nature's seasons flow one into another, sports seasons give way from one to another. With the end of the basketball season, baseball season came into full swing. Seeing the other eight-year-old kids swinging bats and throwing balls put a nervous lump in my throat. Nonetheless, I agreed to play.

I joined the local Giants baseball team. Once again, I was a natural front runner, ending the season with a leading batting average, even though I was the youngest on the team. Soon enough, I found success as a pitcher. Just like I would become a point guard in basketball, (the player who brings the ball up the court and through whom the offense runs), I would learn to take center stage in the baseball diamond.

I was riding a sports high. I didn't set out to be a three-sport player, but once baseball was done, I thought, Why not try my hand at football? And I excelled in it as well.

Though I was in my first year there too, I didn't play like a rookie. Those aren't my words, but the words of my coach. Once again, there I was on center stage, playing none other than quarterback of the Oakcrest team. I still made sure to keep friendships first and have fun.

Weeks and months can seem like forever to a kid, but with the constant fun and thrill of sports, my ninth birthday quickly rolled around, and I was at the start of another basketball season with the Lincoln Park Celtics.

We were a solid team and just gelled with each other. As a matter of fact, our record that year was 10–0. It felt good to be undefeated. No, it felt awesome! I wasn't the only standout as we had great players like James Salvage, Darryl Adams, and Eddie Smith (no relation).

In my second year of balling, I made the Youth All-Star Team of Pensacola. The All-Stars Tournament was held in Orlando. We headed there feeling confident that we would come home with the Youth State Championship.

We were tough and full of swagger, I guess as much swagger as nine year olds could have. We breezed through the first few teams like running through wet tissue paper. This led up to the championship match against Apopka, a local team from just outside of Orlando. We just knew those city boys would be no match for us. Or so we thought. We fought as hard as we could but found ourselves consoling each other on the quiet ride back home. We couldn't believe we lost.

And that is another trade-off. You're gonna take your Ls. That's just part of life, but you can either run from your foes or face them head-on.

Losing is a painful reminder to keep working on your craft.

Instead of pulling our heads inside our shells, just re-lying on talent and what we had always done, we vowed to beat them the next time. Up to this point, I had leaned on my natural ability, but more would be needed. I would have to start working on my weak spots, improving pass-ing, ball-handling, and footwork. I was willing to trade in the pain of defeat for the sweat of hard work and hope-fully, taste victory.

Flowing back into the next baseball season, I laced up to play with the Lincoln Park Red Sox. We were no Bad News Bears, that's for sure. For two years, we remained undefeated. I still led the team as the pitcher. With this group, I would pitch five no-hitters in one season. Once again, my body just fit into the mold of sports. No matter what game it was, I always knew where to put the ball.

Then it was back to football. While I was already a little star in my own right, no one—and I mean no one—was ready for what we witnessed that year. I played for the Mites, but the Mini Mites (the younger league below us) had one member who was a true force to be reckoned with. Not a hurricane or a tornado, but none other than future Hall of Famer and NFL all-time leading rusher, Emmitt Smith.

He was a quiet little fellow with whom I walked home

from practice a few times. What we did on the Mites was nothing compared to what we saw with Emmitt. Even at eight, Emmitt was the talk of the town. He was fast, intelligent, and could fake out anyone on the field. When you watched him move, it was a thing of beauty.

Emmitt was not only playing offense, he became the offense. The Mini Mites really had only two plays, and they led to tremendous success.

1. Hand the ball to Emmitt.
2. Throw the ball to Emmitt.

He would score four or five touchdowns a game. It was not hard to see that he had a great future ahead of him. My time knowing him brought nothing monumental. He was quiet, but he knew how to spend his energy where it counted.

Again, was this a sign of things to come? Was God allowing me to be refined in some way? I didn't get jealous of Emmit's success but rooted for him as so many others had rooted for me. He would certainly not be the last stellar talent that I would come into contact with, and I'm glad to say I knew him a little. Spending time and rubbing shoulders with greatness would become a familiar path.

When I wasn't on the field or court playing with official youth leagues, it was not hard to find me. If I wasn't in school, I was sure to be playing a pickup game of some kind. Because our neighborhood was safe, Momma would gladly send me off to play basketball to get me out of her hair. That security of having a real community meant I could walk back and forth to the park to play at will.

Pickup games can be more than just child's play, a true testament to how great you really are. A random group of friends starts playing and teams evenly divide into two-on-two. That grows to three-on-three and eventually, a group running full-court five-on-five. With no refs or officiating, it's not always fair, and the game can get annoying, depending on who you play with. But it's a good analogy for many things in life where we have to follow a general form and make it up a little as we go along.

You really know you're good when it builds up to five-on-five and fifteen guys are standing on the sidelines, salivating to get in on the next game. In pickup ball, one rule was consistent: winners rule the court, and losers get to stepping. If you're on the losing team, it's back to the sidelines unless whoever goes next wants to pick you up.

Again, playing pickup gave me confirmation of how good I really was. More times than not, even when I happened to be on a losing team, while the other four guys walked away, I stayed on the court because the next group up almost always picked me to be on their team.

Even older players saw my skills and recognized my ability. This was a great blessing because it allowed me to develop even further. Raw, unfiltered balling on the court was almost more of a real game than the organized sports. Pickup games developed real skill. Organized leagues provided a platform to showcase it. Whatever you did off the public court would be shown as developed or underdeveloped in league play.

My dedication to pickup would lead me to rub shoulders with Pensacola basketball greatness. Basketball in our town was associated with the name "Washington" in one way or another. Coach Benny Washington was the noted assistant coach at Woodham High where games were always sold out, and the crowds were always roaring.

Coach Washington was tough and made sure his players were tough. For example, if one of his players missed an open layup, he would immediately pull them out of the game and make them do ten push-ups in front of everyone! His philosophy? If you're gonna embarrass us like that, you need to be embarrassed. Safe to say, his players didn't miss many open layups.

Coach Benny had a sister who was an All-American ballplayer, and his younger brother Glenn was a sharp high school player. Glenn saw my talent while playing pickup games. Though I was in middle school and still honing my craft, Glenn and I became close. But I wasn't living in Woodham High's territory lines, so Coach Benny didn't know me. Being a bold competitor, though, he was a little more than curious about who Glenn was hanging out with.

Coach Benny's calculating demeanor put me on notice. This dude don't like me, I thought. That didn't stop me from spending time with Glenn. I wasn't about to turn down learning all that I could from such a skilled player. I had the shooting touch, but it takes more than that to climb to the top. My natural vision and moves would keep me one step ahead of my opponents for only so long. I needed to work on my dribbling and ball-handling. That's where Glenn came in.

One evening, we were out on the court as usual. I was doing my best to hold my own against the bigger, faster Glenn. While no one could match my shooting touch, he had me bested on footwork. He'd get the ball and have his back to me. Leaning back, he'd sense my positioning and anticipate my defense. Then Glenn spun like a top and in flash was putting a layup in the basket.

Okay, okay, I thought. Bet he won't get me like that again.

Once again, I was guarding him, trying to discern which way he was headed, trying to keep him from going to his right. Steady, focused . . . whoosh! He spun by me again. I had seen the older boys spin around opponents in the high school games, and I just had to add that to my repertoire.

"Glenn, you gotta show me how to do that," I insisted.

"I can't give away my secret recipe!"

"Come on, man! Help me out."

Glenn grinned. "All right. Come here."

Then and there, Glenn started showing me the finer points of dribbling and posting up. I was in awe. I'd seen the high school players do these moves so many times. As younger kids, we tried to imitate it, but our awkward little bodies could not yet match their smooth choreography. I was intent on being more than an observer.

I was a student of the game, and class was in session.

"Okay," Glenn said, "like this." He took the ball and began laying out the finer points of his slick movements and hesitations. As I guarded him, my mind and ears were wide open to any instruction I could get. Soon, the sun had gone down, and twilight had passed. Enraptured by hooping, we paid no attention to darkness. The flickering streetlamp gave enough light for our young eyes.

Then came a call out into the night: "Alfy! Boy, get your tail in here! It's late!"

Momma. Calling me from home.

I pretended like I didn't hear her.

"Boy, don't act like you don't hear me! Get your butt in this house before I have to beat you. You gotta go to school in the morning."

"Momma, I don't care about that! I'm learning how to spin with that ball in my hand."

Let me say I don't believe in not minding your parents, but dedication to my craft had me zeroed in on this training. All I could think was, well, you're gonna have to beat me then 'cause I ain't about to trade in learning how to get these moves down.

Thank goodness, she decided not to give me a whooping! Since I was always well-behaved, I guess she figured it was best to let me play. Playing kept me out of trouble. Plus, I always had my things ready for school in the morning and cleaned up the house every Saturday morning so we would be free to play ball in the afternoon. Just another example of the trade-offs I was willing to make for a chance to rise to the top.

Time for a pause and to break down a lesson. Make sure you take care of life's necessary little things. Talent is no excuse for having an attitude or for chores not being done. Because Momma could rely on me to do what I was supposed to do, she didn't mind me taking that time to play a little later that night. Those kinds of trade-offs are always worth it.

Glenn and I would stay close throughout my middle school years, but I couldn't get over how his older brother didn't seem to like me. I wasn't about to let it bother me. That's just life.

5. Bring Back the Memories

I WAS ENJOYING success on the field and on the court. In baseball, I was killing it as a pitcher. I'd play with the organized youth leagues and turn right around and play with neighborhood leagues. One day at the Salvation Army Park, I struck out twelve batters, changed uniforms, went to Bill Gregory Park to play with the neighborhood group, and struck out another thirteen batters! I was spitting hot fire!

At age ten, I was playing my final season with the Lincoln Park Celtics basketball team where we went an undefeated 10–0. I was once again voted to the Youth All-Star Team of Pensacola. This meant heading back to Orlando where we were sure we would win the championship this time. We had a score to settle.

Last year's loss remained fresh in our minds. Would we have what it takes to win it all this year? Had we put in enough effort to overcome our weaknesses? Or were we just overconfident? Once I had jumped on the sports train, I was determined to make it a way of life, and that meant the constant dedication and trade-offs that would hopefully lead to payoffs.

We arrived at the tournament with pure focus. We had our minds set, ready to go through a run similar run to the previous year. We mentally prepared to dust off a couple of lesser opponents and bring our absolute best to the championship. Looking at the schedule, our jaws dropped.

We were sure the schedulers were out to get us. There, listed as our first game, was Apopka, the team who beat us in the championship last year! There were to be no warm-up games, just a championship rematch right out of the gate.

I looked around at my frazzled teammates. "Guys, we got this. It don't matter if we play Apopka, Ozarker, or whoever: we're gonna win this!" This was no time to show fear, but to face the course with determination.

Apopka was confident as well, and why not? They had handled us last year, so they assumed they were in for a cakewalk.

We suited up and took our places on the court, ready for jump ball. After a moment's pause, the whistle blew.

The game was on, and from start to finish, Apopka knew they were in trouble.

We would not be denied this year. We wiped the floor with Apopka and went on to win the overall tournament. As the old saying goes, "there is no 'I' in team," and it was truly a team effort. We all gave our best, and that's the only way we won.

A fine lesson: always work as a team. Rely on your teammates. Trust in your team. Even in solo sports like tennis or boxing, a team surrounds the athlete to raise their game and keep them operating at their peak.

I learned the importance of sticking to valued teammates like brothers. Insisting on being a team player allowed me to shine as an individual. I made the all-tournament team with James Wright and Artie Mc'cover. If that wasn't reward enough, my name was published in the Orlando Sentinel newspaper for the accomplishment. The accolades didn't stop there. On arrival back in Pensacola, I was lauded for my on-court effectiveness. I was gob smacked to hear the WBOP radio report: "And here's congratulating our own Pensacola Youth All-Stars for bringing home the State Championship. A special congratulations go to Alfy Smith who won the MVP. We see a lot of great things in store for that young man."

Woo! I was on top of the world. Then they gave me a three-day excused absence from school. You know I was all about that! My teammates and I were each awarded a championship jacket.

My star was on the rise.

That year turned out especially good for Pensacola because a local high school team, Washington High, won the Boys' State Championship. We younger kids felt like we were really something because we happened to be staying at the same hotel as they were.

Basketball was becoming my sole sports focus which marked another trade-off soon to come. At each rising level in sports, the talent becomes stiffer, and you have to make greater leaps in your ability. I was still succeeding on the baseball diamond and football field, but my gifts were only just a bit above average in those domains.

I had transitioned from quarterback to running back in football. No longer in the lead role, I was still a crucial member of the offense. That led me to another distinction: the slowest running back in the league! (Cue the trombones.) But it didn't mean I was a failure. I may have been slower than the others, but hardly anyone could tackle me! I always seemed to have a gift for anticipation and knowing how to escape. I would juke the opponent out of their shoes and leave them on the ground. I knew how to hesitate—right, left—and then pop out of the way for a clean break. Remember to use what you've got to your advantage. You're not always going to be the tallest or fastest but use what you've got.

It makes me think of the great Michael Jordan. His speed and shooting skill weren't enough to go through heavier, rougher opponents and win championships. He had to build muscle to pound his way through. He developed a deadlier and deadlier jump shot. And as age slowed him a half-step, he crafted an unstoppable fadeaway shot.

Always work on sharpening your craft.

I'd be remiss not to continue mentioning the valuable role family played. Just because I was gaining a little local fame didn't mean Momma was gonna totally spoil me. Same rules applied as before, chores had to be done Saturday morning before we could go out and play any ball. All the while, Grandmomma was my biggest supporter, making sure the whole family knew about my games and bragging on me to no end.

So things were perfect, right?

Well, trade-offs have their pain, and not everyone will be happy for your success. I would soon learn this all too well.

6. Competition

GETTING WOUNDED PHYSICALLY, emotionally, or any other way is an inevitable part of life. A close strike to our vital organs causes the most pain, and the deepest emotional wounds come from those closest to you. When you cheer for others, you presume that others will cheer for you. At least, that's what I believed. Unfortunately, that's not always the case, and once, emotional hurt almost stole the day.

I was twelve years old and hooping more and more each day with the Wedgewood Middle School team. I took pride in not only being a high-volume scorer but in being a good teammate. I certainly was not a ball hog trying to pump up my own stat line.

Whenever my teammates scored, I celebrated along with the crowd. Each defensive stop from a blocked shot or a stolen ball brought me sincere joy. I would clap my hands and shout, "Way to go!" and high-five my team-mates. But I began to notice the cheers weren't coming back my way so readily. I was scoring a lot, so it wasn't for lack of opportunity.

I still hadn't come to grips with the fact that jealousy in sports is an unfading constant. My popularity was on the rise with my classmates but on the decline with my teammates. It came to a head with one great honor that I didn't expect.

The cover of the yearbook was typically reserved for the school mascot. But that year, my exploits on the court led the yearbook committee to put me on the cover with Sam Robinson and Lori Jamerson on the cover of the yearbook. Come on, man, who would imagine? We were undefeated again at 10–0 with no signs of slowing down.

But a deep wound was festering in the team. One day after practice, Coach summoned me to his office.

This was odd, so I was a little shaky. "Coach, I had a message to come see you."

Coach understood my nerves and responded in a warm tone. "Alfy, I want you to know that you are my best player, and without you, there's no way we'd be un-defeated."

I sensed a hammer was about to drop, and it was gonna drop right on top of me. My throat tightened up, and I quickly stammered, "Coach, whatever it is, I promise you, I did not do it."

Coach got a little more serious, ready to cut to the chase. "Alfy, no. It's nothing like that. You're not in trouble. Alfy, look, I don't know how to say this, but the team is a little upset with you because you're scoring most of the points."

What? My mind started racing. That's why they were being so cold. I couldn't stand it. I had never been used to anything but encouragement up to that point. I faced a trade-off that I wasn't ready to make. I loved sports, but more than anything else, I loved seeing people happy. I hated to be the source of pain. All I was doing was trying to be my best for my team, and that's how they felt?

I was done. "Coach, I don't wanna play no more. I will just—"

"I don't wanna hear that," Coach interrupted sternly. "You're gonna play. But this is what I want you to do: When you score twenty points, start passing the ball. Pull back on your scoring. Understand?"

"Yes sir," I sputtered softly.

I don't tend to get angry, but my conversation with the coach changed something in me that day. I was mad.

It led to one thought: I'll show you. I felt so unappreciated, and in my frustration and anger, I devised a plan.

The next game put us up against Bellview Middle School. Bellview beating Wedgewood would be like Steve Urkel knocking out Mike Tyson in a boxing match, so we were pretty secure in our standing. It was Monday night, and the game was about to begin. The crowd rumbled with excitement, ready to see us show out.

The game got going, and I ran the point as usual. I brought the ball up and zipped it over to the first open man I saw. As play continued, I kept up the pattern, bring the ball up, pass. Bring the ball up, pass. With two minutes left in the first quarter, Bellview was up by four points, 11–7. Now, keep in mind we had never trailed against this team. Normally, we would be up by ten or fifteen points.

When play resumed for the second quarter, the ball was inbounded to me, and I passed it to another player. He took a shot and clank, a miss. Bellview scuttled to rebound, passing the ball until a clean shot was up and good.

Play continued this way through the remainder of the first half. I'd get the ball with an easy, open look, but instead of taking the shot, I'd pass the ball to another player.

My teammates finally started to notice my disengagement; we were losing to a team that we should be blowing out. You could hear our fans moan in the stands every time I passed the ball. From the faint buzz of conversation, you could tell they knew something is up.

"What's wrong with him? Why doesn't he shoot it?"

The tension grew thicker and thicker. My teammates started pleading with me.

"Shoot it, Alfy!"

"Come on, take the shot!"

"All you, Alfy!"

But each time I got the ball, I shoved it away to a teammate like it was Kryptonite.

The first half came to a close with the score Bellview thirty, Wedgewood twenty. I had zero points on zero shot attempts.

My good friend, Pookie, was irate at my deliberate underperforming. "Hey yo, Al! You better start shooting the #$%@ ball!"

I smirked, shrugged, and ran into the dressing room. As Coach berated the team for our performance, I sat there silent, just nodding along. This is what y'all wanted, I thought. How do you like it now?

As we approached the second half, my teammates

were still encouraging me to shoot, and I continued to refuse. Onlookers were in shock. Bellview, the worst team in the district, was beating one of the best. Bellview had no complaints, and they took full advantage. With two minutes left in the third quarter, they were stomping us, leading by fifteen.

By then, Coach and my teammates were screaming at me to shoot, begging, imploring. That's what I wanted. I needed them to recognize my contribution to the team. With that accomplished, all engines engaged, I went to work.

At the end of the third, we were down by ten points. The fourth quarter began, and that familiar shooting touch was on. The lead was cut, and Bellview began to panic. After counting me out, they had to scramble to preserve what would have been their greatest bragging right.

Not today, boys.

The game was tied in short order as I kept up my stroke. When all was said and done, in just one quarter and a half, I had scored twenty-two points. A high for most players in a whole game, much less a third of one.

Mission accomplished. After that game, my team-mates never mumbled another word about me shooting the ball.

So what's the takeaway? Work through emotions. Plan and implement. Prove your worth. That day, I learned to work through my emotions, handle a situation, and then let it go, finding a way to replace good feelings for bad.

In life, we are always competing in some form or another. That's the truth. But to live a healthy life, we must realize competitors are not the enemy. It takes maturity and humility to embrace that concept. If we choose to view our competitors as something lesser, as enemies, we can only suffer. From that standpoint, we must leave personal feelings about competitors and teammates on the field. There are bigger things in life than sports. The day you lose a loved one or a cherished opportunity, those supposed enemies don't seem so bad as they once did.

Keep your friends and loved ones, your teammates and associates close. Never fail to tell them how you feel about them, because one day it may be too late. But above all, trade pride for teamwork, grief for joy, and hate for love. Leave it all on the field.

7. School

I ONLY SOUGHT to give the game my best, and for that, I was rewarded. Some things were out of my control, but what I could control, I did to the best of my ability. I showed love to my family and respect on the court to coaches and teammates. I always practiced hard and kept a winning attitude.

Without a father in the house to help develop my skill and nurture it, I relied on the coaches who came through and supported me. For this, I send a shout out to all the coaches who help develop fatherless children in their communities. That spirit led me to make coaching a key part of my life to this day, whether for work or as a volunteer. I ended up majoring in Physical Education and continue to coach and train kids. I gladly became a father figure to many others because of this.

As I moved into high school, I continued to reap the

fruitage of being a gifted athlete. The more I put into basketball, the more that I recognized it as something greater to me than a sport; it was a passion. Football and baseball went to the side so I could give basketball all my focus.

The two powerhouse teams in the area were the Pensacola Tigers and the Washington Wildcats, and that remains true today. Both teams are known for aggressive play and high-flying, slam-dunking style that built winning histories. To play against either was to count on an L for your team.

I attended Pine Forest High, so I was an Eagle. We had the confidence and the talent to believe that we could beat any team on any given night. Bring on the Wildcats and the Tigers! We were not to be contained.

Back in the day, those were blasphemous words, but words we wholeheartedly believed. Knowing the challenges I would face, I vowed neither Washington nor Pensacola High would beat any team I was on. Maybe that was some youthful arrogance, but for the trade-off to reach the payoff, one needs to believe in oneself to push for the dedication required and embrace lofty goals.

In my freshman year, I had the skills to play on the varsity team, but out of respect for the senior players, I was relegated to the junior varsity squad. (Coincidentally, a similar thing happened to the great Michael Jordan.) This position in a lesser league must have been disheartening for some of my opponents because it was easier for me to dominate the game. Yet, the experience allowed me to demonstrate humility and the willingness to be a team player. I accepted the assignment as all others. To the surprise of no one, I led the team in scoring. Still, the greatest joy came in beating our top rivals, especially a major school nemesis.

I'll cut to the chase. The game was tied with fifteen seconds to go. We had possession of the ball, and Coach drew up the play for me to take the last shot. As I look back, I'm sure that probably didn't sit well with the older players, but it is what it is. The coach believed in me, and I knew I wouldn't let the team down.

The ball was inbounded, and the rapid chirping of sneakers bounced off the hardwood floor. The ball was being passed around quickly.

Ten seconds to go.

Both coaches were pacing and shouting out orders. The ball finally made its way to me.

Five seconds.

My opponent was on me like white on rice, but there

was no time to hesitate.

Three seconds.

I rose up and released the ball just like I always did over the outstretched hands of my defender. All eyes were on the ball sailing towards the basket. With a lovely backspin, it glided and glided and . . . swish! The crowd was on their feet, and our opponents dropped their heads. We raised our hands in the air. We, the Pine Forest Eagles, toppled the mighty Washington Wildcats!

While I overachieved in basketball, I underachieved in academics—only because I didn't fully apply myself. I had the ability, but I was too caught up in basketball to have the motivation to do any more than just skate by with the bare minimum in class.

I urge young folks to not make that same mistake but to maximize all of your talents and get a balanced education. The truth is, even a long career in the sports world will rarely take you as much as halfway through your life. Gain the skills you need to contribute something more to society. There are so many opportunities today that we didn't have. Please seize them.

Sophomore year marked my passage to the varsity team. We proclaimed ourselves the best in the city, and we were destined for greatness. Only time would tell. We backed it up by starting the season as the proud owners of an undefeated record, 6–0. Piece of cake. Next up: Tate High. No match for us, we ran through them like a hot knife through butter. Seven–zero.

Then we faced a powerhouse on their home court: the Pensacola Tigers. Game night arrived, and it was time to ball. In the pregame speech, Coach pumped us up and firmly repeated the necessary reminders. "I want you to play hard. If you're open, shoot the ball. If you're not open, pass the ball to the open man. No hurried or rushed shots, okay? Huddle up. On three: 'Defenses.'"

Then he barked like a drill sergeant: "One, two, three . . ."

"Defenses!" we all shouted and headed out to the gym.

The bleachers were jam-packed. We were simply overwhelmed by the crowd in the stands. The Pensacola Tigers flaunted the pride that came with bearing the town name, and they ran onto the floor with a mighty roar from the crowd. Their warm-ups were nothing short of impressive.

But now the clock was set, and it was time to get down to it.

Despite being on hostile territory, we did not waver in confidence. We stuck to our principles, fundamentals, and belief in ourselves. What we believed, we proved, and when the clock clicked to 0:00, there we were, the last men standing. Eagles 76, Tigers 60. Victory, 8–0, and we were on a roll.

Our next opponent gave us no time to rest because, again, we faced a nemesis: the Washington Wildcats. It was a home game for us, and the student body was fired up. I could just feel it. It was the most important game of the year. Washington sat at the pinnacle of the local basketball world, and a victory over them would cement us as true contenders and not pretenders.

With their pedigree of local dominance and history of championships, the Wildcats had a well-deserved reputation for trash talk. That night would be no exception. My teammates and I locked into the task at hand. Coach made sure to remind us that our undefeated status—our ZERO—was on the line.

Jump ball. The whistle blew, and the game began. I wish I could give you some remarkable play of the action, but sadly (for the Wildcats), there wasn't much to relay. We dominated from start to finish. Our crowd was losing their minds with joy.

With one quarter left in the game, the score was Home: 73, Visitors: 51. We were about to defeat the mighty Wildcats, a feat by a smaller local school not heard of. The fourth quarter started, and we quickly scored three times to bring the score to 79–51.

Then the magic happened.

Someone in the crowd stood up and waved a dollar bill. Others in the stands took notice and began to do the same. That custom challenged you to score one hundred points against your opponents. Now, you show the best sportsmanship by not running up the score when your opponents are clearly outmatched, but the Wildcats were cocky coming in, and sometimes a message needs to be sent. Class was in session, and we were about to school them.

Any fatigue we felt melted away. The engagement of our fans energized us, and our faith rose from believing we could achieve victory to believing we could hit one hundred points. With three minutes left, the score was 91–57. We were just having our way with the kitty cats— excuse me, Wildcats.

Aware of the crowd taunting them, and wanting to avoid having their pride totally crushed, the Wildcats called a time out. Usually, the winning team would hold onto the ball to stall and eat up time on the clock to assure a victory while the losing team rushed to score as much as possible in hopes of a comeback. But the roles were reversed. The Wildcats held the ball, stalling, praying they wouldn't have to go back to their school with their tails between legs after we dropped one hundred points on them.

Well, their prayers went unanswered that night. In just under two minutes, we raised our score 99–61. Despite all their bragging and swagger, the Wildcats were prone to making mistakes, and we took advantage.

We quickly devised a time-honored strategy to get the ball back. We would deliberately foul their players, forcing them into free throws, and returning us possession of the ball. The crowd was mercilessly screaming and waving one-dollar bills.

With less than a minute to go, we had possession of the ball once again. Some swift passes and the ball ended up in my hands. Racing against the clock, I leaped into the air and released the ball.

Up and good!

The whole crowd and the players went totally berserk. People jumped up and down and gave each other high fives. Bass notes and a victorious tune thumped over the loudspeakers: Another One Bites the Dust by Queen.

The final score: Wildcats 63, the Mighty Eagles 101.

Scoring over one hundred in high school is always a rare feat.

As I walked off the court celebrating with my best friend from way back, Brian Thompson (aka Bird), people stuffed dollar bills into my hand. I collected them and joyfully handed them over to Bird. It was sweet, sweet victory, again!

After this big win, we thought we were unstoppable. Well. Youth is often defined by its lack of experience. It's good to have confidence, but you can't get too high on yourself. Within the same week, we suffered back-to-back losses from the Catholic Crusaders and the Woodham Titans, where the assistant coach was none other than Benny Washington. In fact, they defeated us handily. It must have taught us something because we rebounded against the Escambia Gators, home of the great Emmitt Smith. I hate to say it, but it was a close game. Still, I had a chance to show that neither our team nor I had lost nerve. Like many times before, I rose up to hit the winning bucket.

We ended the season 24–4 and were crowned district champs. USA Today ranked us twenty-fourth in the whole nation. Out of thousands of schools, we were in the highest reaches of sports greatness. We eventually became sectional champs and regional runners-up.

In the regional game, we had another hard-fought battle. We faced the cream of the crop. With the clock winding down, the ball was in my hands. I let it rip, and it went sailing, sailing, and . . . clank. My heart sank. Maybe it was fatigue. I don't believe it was pressure. We couldn't make them all. At least we had seen the heights and brought pride to the school.

No matter the pain of that defeat, I traded off misery for being joyful and hopeful over what we had done.

The difficulty with high school ball and college ball is the team changes every year, sometimes drastically so. Seniors leave, and freshmen come in. Junior varsity members move up and chemistry shifts suddenly. My individual numbers were great as usual, but as a team, we lacked competitiveness in my junior and senior years. Those seasons were nothing more than average.

I didn't lack inspiration or lose any love for the game. It was around this time that I began to notice the rise of someone who I would admire greatly along with the rest of the world. Michael Jordan was making a name for himself. Mike was amazing to watch. I sat with mouth agape at his aerial acrobatics and his ability to just will the ball into the hoop.

I was on my momma's couch one day watching Mike's UNC Tar Heels against Wake Forest. Mike was conducting a clinic. In one instant, Mike wove through traffic, and in a flash, he was in the air and wham dunked over three players.

I was in such shock I audibly cursed with my momma right there.

"Boy!" she laughed, swatting at me.

"Sorry, Momma," I sheepishly muttered.

Like a machine programmed to process basketball, I assimilated Mike's moves and began to imitate them in my game as best I could, figuring how to attack the double team without fear.

High school was full of good times besides basketball. Like a lot of folks, I had dreams of performing on stage, and I've always loved music. I don't have the best singing voice, but it's deep and when I do a spoken verse in love ballads, people tell me I sound like Mike from Boys II Men.

My favorite group of all time broke out in fame while I was in high school: the one, the only New Edition! To this day, I love their music. It carried me in times of pain and became the soundtrack to some of my happiest memories.

At the Pine Forest High Variety Show, I joined a group called True Edition with my boys Brian Thompson, Charles Cepris, Wayne Fort, and Sean Salter. I was the last member of True Edition like my buddy Ronnie Devote was the last member of New Edition. I was supposed to start the routine off. I've never been one to have nerves in front of a crowd, but a trained singer I am not. So once I stepped out on the stage and peered into the crowd, my heart fired like a jackhammer! Without thinking, I turned myself right back around and went to the end of the line. But I wasn't gonna run away from it even though I was embarrassed. We started the routine over again. We still get a good laugh out of that.

And like I said, while I had my own successes, I was always proud of otherworldly talent in our hometown when I saw it. Remember little Emmitt Smith from the Mini Mites? Well, he was now a star running back for Escambia High. One Friday night, I went to see my own Pine Forest Eagles take on the Escambia Gators.

I sat at the top of the bowl-shaped stadium and noticed things hadn't changed much from Mini Mites days. The Gators could rely on two unstoppable plays:

1. Hand the ball to Emmitt.
2. Pass the ball to Emmitt.

Emmitt was on his way to become the second leading rusher in high school football history. He transformed Escambia from a school with only one winning season in football to a division and state champion. This night proved no exception to his greatness.

I hated to see our Eagles lose, but Emmitt was outstanding! On one play, he got the ball from the QB and headed straight towards a linebacker down in tackle position. Emmitt didn't flinch. Instead of cutting, spinning, or juking, he just jumped, up, up, up . . . clear over the linebacker's head! He landed, cut left, and made his way to the end zone.

The stadium exploded in cheers. All I could think was, that is the best play I have ever seen in my life! Of course, Emmitt would go on to much bigger things.

In a blink, it was already graduation. We boys felt like men. At least we thought we were. On the eve of my graduation, my friend Alvin Wiggins (aka Lil Cat) and I decided to purchase a twelve-pack of Milwaukee's Best. (Remember, this was back when the legal drinking age was not yet raised to twenty-one.) We called this our pre-graduation celebration. We were laughing, talking, and having a good time.

Well, when the day of commencement arrived, I was

unbalanced, my speech was slurred, and my motor skills were slow as well. Say it in a low voice: I was buzzed! As the ceremony began, my head spun. But it was still a big day for me, a momentous occasion, time to get that diploma.

The *S* section made its progression toward the front of the stage. One by one, each student was called to receive his or her diploma. When my name was called, though impaired, I managed to walk across the stage without falling. I'm not sure what the principal thought when he saw me, but I shook his hand, flashed a megawatt smile for the audience, and stumbled off the stage.

Dizzy and unbalanced, I attempted to locate my seat. Finally, I sat down, thinking I was cool, and nobody had noticed my condition. I soon found out that at the supposedly dignified event, I had taken the wrong seat, completely disrupting the entire seating order. I couldn't help but giggle.

At least I learned to not drink too much. You think you can fool folks, but you're only fooling yourself!

8. Crucial

WHILE I WAS able to enjoy great local success, another star was rising far above where I could personally reach, but I would shortly have the chance to rocket alongside. Roy Jones, Jr. was honing his craft in the boxing world. We were from different sides of town and a few years different in age, so I never really knew him growing up. Still, the success of any one of Pensacola's own was a reason for me to take pride.

Living in a small city meant we would bump into the same people without ever getting to know each other. Sean Desoto was an old friend of mine and a local sports star who sparred with eleven-year-old Roy just as I was starting my high school basketball career. Sean saw the spark of greatness in Roy and announced to all that Roy would be a world champion one day. I didn't take an overwhelming interest in Roy at that point, but whenever the hometown boy did good, I had a mild rooting interest in his success.

College was a major pivot point in my life as it is for all young adults. I started at Concordia Junior College in Selma, Alabama. Of course, my focus wasn't so much academic as it was basketball related. The only natural fit for me would be to pursue a major in physical education, keeping my focus and values in the sports world.

At Concordia, I continued to be the star player on the school team. As a smaller school, we were only allowed six games in the first half of the season compared to the fourteen games given to other schools. Still, I ended up being the lead scorer for the first half of that season.

At one point during a tournament in Selma, we were down by twenty points. I couldn't bear being beaten so badly without a real fight. Something seized inside me, and I got to work. I started shooting and hit eight jumpers in a row without a miss. *Bang! Bang! Bang!* I was a sharp-shooter that night, which may be why one of my high school nicknames had been Al Capone. I ended that game with thirty-eight points—without taking a single three-point shot because they didn't yet exist in college ball!

Still on a roll, I scored twenty-two the next night. The following week I hung twenty-nine on Patrick Henry

Junior College. Terry Sellers, their coach, was furious at the whooping I laid on them. Finally, in a rage, Coach Sellers glared over at his point guard, Jeff McCoy, and barked, "If Alfy Smith hits another shot, I want you to punch him right in the mouth!"

Well, cooler heads prevailed, and I didn't get punched that night. We were able to continue our run for a couple more games before being knocked out of the tournament, and I was honored to be given the All-Tournament trophy.

Sadly, I ran into a familiar obstacle: jealousy. Other players thought I was scoring too many points. This time there was no convincing anyone differently through trickery on the court, and we didn't have the bonds of being lifelong neighbors to move us past the roadblock.

For better or worse, I made the decision to transfer to none other than Patrick Henry Junior College in Monroeville, Alabama. I'd be playing under Coach Sellers himself! I had heard the story about his order to Jeff and had to ask him about it.

"Hey, Coach!"

"Yeah, Alfy?"

"Did you really tell Jeff McCoy if I hit another shot to punch me in the mouth?"

Coach barely hesitated before spitting out: "Well, you

weren't missing!"

I couldn't help but laugh. We all get a little out of hand sometimes over our passions.

The trade-off of changing schools came with a price. In a transfer like that, eligibility to continue to play ball was determined by the president of the shunned school. Upset at my decision to go to a rival, the president of Concordia would not approve me to play with Patrick Henry, so I sat out a year.

That did nothing to diminish my love of the game. The importance of pickup games was once again of great value in my life. When I was allowed to suit up for Patrick Henry the next year, I continued a streak of dominant scoring, but this time with the support of a loyal coach and good teammates.

In fact, their support led me to an opportunity to demonstrate a lack of prejudice and love for all. I hit it off well with a couple of white students, Lee and John, who had gone to an all-white academy before college. Amazed by my abilities on the court, they would call and tell their parents "Alfy this" and "Alfy that." Well, their parents couldn't help but want to meet the famous Alfy, and I ended up spending the night at both of their houses. I must have been the first Black man to cross their thresholds to stay the night!

With racial tensions still not resolved in this day and age, I'm proud to say it again and I've always believed it: I don't care who you are, Black, White, Mexican, Russian, Chinese, Filipino—whatever. If you do right by me, we're brothers. Even if you don't, I'm still gonna show you respect. Also, while at Patrick Henry, I made good friends with Lloyd Patrick, the only Black guy I knew who was a fan of the Boston Celtics, and we always had a good time together.

Too soon, my time at Patrick Henry came to an end. After completing junior college, I moved on to complete my college career at Faulkner University. Although they were once my rivals, when I said my goodbyes to both Coach Sellers and Lloyd, they had tears in their eyes.

At Faulkner, old challenges returned. The coach there didn't really give me much of a shot, and I had to ride the bench. Once, during practice, I stole the ball and scored on the other end. Frustrated at the first team for not doing as well as he thought they should, Coach blew up at me, telling me I was somehow cheating.

That was the last straw. I was always known for getting along with anyone, but the lack of respect was too much. I blew up at the coach. That shocked everyone since I had a reputation for being peaceable. I stormed off, and I'm not proud to say I threw a stool in anger as Coach continued berating me. In the locker room, I was prepared to fight him, but thankfully it never came to that. I was ready to go home right then. By this point, I had twin baby girls I could have been working to feed. What was I doing riding the bench? Was this the right trade-off?

Eventually, the dust settled, and the team understood my passion. Come senior year, my talents were recognized by the new coach, Tom Kelsey. I became star point guard and was able to get a few more highlights.

A memorable game came when unexpectedly Momma showed up with my two girls. Wanting to impress all three of them, I changed the plays coach had called. First, I called one that set me up on the left side for a corner three. *Swish.* Next time down the court, I called another play that set me up on the right side for a corner three. *Swish.* Finally, on our next play with the ball, I called a play for a teammate, Ted, who drilled a three. *Swish.*

Coach sat there stunned. Next time out, he called me over and said, "Alfy, from now on, you can call whatever plays you want!"

I averaged ten points, 2.7 rebounds, 2.5 steals, and 5.3 assists a game over my college career. I was on fire again, and scouts would soon be coming to check us out for a possible pro career overseas. But just like a sudden tropical storm can change course and hit us here in the Gulf, dark changes swiftly turned my world upside down.

Six games into the season, at a practice just before our game against Troy State, my roommate Chris Johns reached to grab the ball from me. As I swept it out of his reach, I heard a *pop*. Fire swelled through my right hand centered on my index finger. I clutched at the ball, holding it carefully, and a strange sense of worry gripped me. I tried to get the ball down the court, but I struggled as if I had never held one before.

"Alfy, you all right?" a teammate asked.

"Man, my finger, I don't know!" I replied in a trembling voice.

I tried to shake it off like we were always told to try to do back in those days. The team manager wrapped up my finger, but it wasn't feeling any better. Reluctantly, I went to the hospital the next day and waited impatiently for the x-rays to come back.

When they finally did, I heard a word that would be devastating for any athlete: *broken*.

What? I was right at the cusp of something big, that moment in time when recruiters called schools to check out talent for pro teams. A broken finger meant I would miss the rest of the season. There would be no tape of my prowess and no YouTube videos to share my highlights.

What a disaster. In an instant, all my dreams of a pro career in the U.S. or overseas were shattered.

I sank into a mild depression. Still having the optimism of youth, I thought that somehow, someway, an opportunity to turn things around would come. Expectation postponed is the mother of all frustration, and there would be more disappointments I couldn't yet fathom. I was still learning to face the facts: even when bad things come at you back to back, you cannot allow them to define who you are. You have to trade pain for positivity.

I came to a huge fork in my road. Great choices were to be made. An opportunity to move up or move down was coming, and I had no way to anticipate it. Until this point, my trade-offs had only limited consequences, the decisions of a child and youth. Coming into my own as a man, the stakes rose, and consequences would be more substantial. Clouds were gathering for one of many storms.

Could I stand the rain long enough to see sunshine again?

Time would reveal the answer.

9. Can You Stand the Rain?

AS I WAS finishing up college, I became something of a fallen leaf tossed wherever the breeze would take me. I thought I would at least be able to finish up my schooling, and with a degree in Phys Ed, I could make a living and find some other way into the basketball world. Being naive like most of us are in our youth, I would soon learn the power of minding who you run with and in turn, gain a greater appreciation for keeping good friends.

As I mentioned, I didn't know Roy Jones, Jr. personally at that time, but as my college career drew to a close, Roy was making a greater name for himself in the boxing world. When I was back home in Pensacola, Roy would sometimes be in the stands while we played ball at Cobbs Center. I had no idea that Roy had a real love for basketball. Boxing was his career, but basketball was his true passion.

The summer before senior year at Faulkner, I was watching the Olympics like most folks, eager to see the hometown boy make us proud. It was the world stage and Pensacola was in the house; Roy Jones was finally battling for the gold.

Friend and teammate Kevin Mixon watched the fight with me. Roy was brilliant! From start to finish he controlled and dominated the fight. Ray Charles and Stevie Wonder could have seen he was the clear winner.

But the fix was in. The Olympics were in South Korea that year, and conveniently, South Korean boxer Park Si-Hun was Roy's competition. Roy wiped the floor with him, landing nearly triple the punches. Yet, everyone was shocked—even the ref and Park Si-Hun himself—when the judges awarded Park the gold as the winner of the match.

Kevin and I sat speechless for a moment. When I looked at Kevin to voice my disbelief, I saw angry tears rolling down his face. I was ready to slam the TV off. Shoot, I was ready to throw the TV through the window, but we sat and watched, taking in the aftermath like the carnage of a train wreck you hate to see but can't look away from.

At the medal ceremony, they placed the silver medallion around Roy's neck. He promptly took it off and never wore it again. In an interview later, he said that he might never box again.

Roy's frustration burned inside me too.

As the end of senior year approached, my finger had healed up, but the season in my life for a basketball career was long over. Though I was down over missed opportunities, I continued my efforts to be a friend to everyone. I love basketball more than everything except people.

Well, it's not always the best course to be close to everyone. The Bible says a "companion of fools will come to harm." A kid named Jason was known for getting in trouble, but he seemed harmless to me. We had a couple classes together, so I was friendly to him. One day, he told me about a going-away party he was going to have and asked if I could get some weed for him because he had just gotten robbed. I felt bad for him, and being young and foolish, I agreed. I won't lie; I have tried the stuff but didn't really like it. Like I said before, I prefer the natural high of life on the court.

I got the weed and met up with Jason who had someone else along. The guy who came with him wouldn't look me in the eyes, and that gave me a funny feeling about the situation. After we made what would have normally been a friendly exchange, the other guy flashed a badge.

My heart hit the floor, and my stomach practically turned inside out.

Fast-forward to interrogation. Even in that tight spot, I couldn't help but be helpful. I respected the police and had no ill will to a man doing his job. I mean, I got myself in this situation so there was no turning back.

As the detective who made the arrest grilled me, I had to let him know something.

"Hey," I said. "I ain't trying to tell you how to do your job, but just FYI, when you do this, you gotta make sure you look people in the eye, or you might get hurt. Some of these brothers will know something's up."

Taken aback, the investigator paused for a second, thought about it, and then flipped open his personal notebook. He wrote it down. He could sense my sincerity and helpfulness. I wasn't holding back or excusing myself. Later at the trial, he commented about how helpful I had been.

I didn't feel overly worried at that point, just disappointed and wondering how I would handle the situation and explain it to Momma. Back home in Pensacola, the first offense with a little weed like this was a misdemeanor and a fine, so I was ready to pay my penance.

I spent one night in holding and was bailed out. I headed back home and started playing pickup games waiting for my court date. And who should be out on the court but the pride of Pensacola and the real gold medalist, Roy Jones, Jr.

Same pickup rules applied as when we were kids; two captains take turns picking players. Roy started. (Who's gonna tell Roy he can't pick first?) To my surprise, he said, "I got Big Al."

Now, I'd never played with Roy before, but obviously, he respected my skills. Despite all my accolades and awards, I was excited. Roy Jones, Jr., a world-famous boxer, respected my game!

We got to hooping, and it was intense like street ball should be. We were kicking butt and taking names— the usual for me. During one game, an opposing player shined on Jones and started talking trash. Not one to back down, I shouted to Roy, "Yo, get that n****r back!"

Roy shot me a look with a huge grin. "Now that's what I've been missing!" He had a fire lit under him that day. As I commented before, Roy's father, Big Roy, provided skilled and steady guidance to train Roy in boxing, but Big Roy could be hard and intense. That strength helped build Roy, but at this crossroads for him, he needed encouragement and a friend, someone who would build him up.

Our roles fit perfectly.

At the end of that day, Roy asked me, "Hey yo, Big. Do Spare Tire [our friend Dennis Clanton] know where you live?"

"Yeah," I said.

"Good. I'll pick you up around nine tomorrow to ball again."

And that marked the start of a beautiful friendship.

But my trial was still awaiting. I headed back up to Montgomery to face my sentence. Like I said, this was normally a misdemeanor fine in Pensacola, so I wasn't overly worried.

But this wasn't Pensacola. This was Montgomery, and traces of the Old South are gonna take time to fully wash away. The eighties were the fiery start of the war on drugs, and while noble in its stated purpose, overly harsh sentences came at the expense of young Black males who some judges and politicians wanted to make an example of.

Had I been on trial just a day later, I would have stood before the Honorable Eugene Reese, a fair and reasonable man, in my opinion. However, on my trial date, the bench was held by Mark "No Deal" Montiel. The sentence was what they called "five years, split three," meaning three years of lockup if you showed good behavior.

Stunned, I headed off to the Montgomery County holding cell where I sat head in hands, thinking what I shared at the beginning of the book. *How did I end up here? God, if you get me out of this, I'm willing to trade whatever I need to do better and take care of my family.*

I was desperate and felt somewhat hopeless.

As I mentioned, I wasn't going to let this ruin me. Let me say to all my brothers and sisters and nephews and nieces who are incarcerated: don't let a minor setback hold you back. When you get hit with an unexpected bump in the road and have to pay a price, whether deserved or unfair, don't lose your edge. Keep the will to pursue better things.

Fortunately, with good behavior, time in the holding cell was only a few months. Just like at home, I always kept everything neat and clean. The guards couldn't help but notice that I was willing to make the best of a bad situation.

And per usual, when we played ball in the yard, I was a standout. Every chance allowed, even by myself, I'd be on the court shooting. Guards would just stop and watch me from their posts or on monitors draining threes, probably betting to see how long I could go before I missed one.

It's a sad fact that the time in the jail was really just a chance for guards to watch and see if you would mess up so that they could make an example of you. One of the grizzled guards looked at me one day as just another wasted youth and said, "I see 'em come and go."

I looked up and snapped back. "But I bet you'll never see me in here again."

My good behavior paid off. I was sent to the Bryce Institute, which was a drug rehab facility and mental hospital. It's what you could call minimum security. Instead of sitting in cells, we had dorms with more freedom to roam around. Still, mess up once, and they would throw your butt back in jail. Right off the bat, in the first month, I got an award for keeping the cleanest dorm. The staff always commented on how nice I was. All my drug tests were clean. They could tell I didn't belong there.

After a few months, I was up for a probationary hearing. I got to stand before a man who was like a saint in my eyes, Judge Reese. Letters of recommendation had been sent on my behalf from guards at the jail, the staff at Bryce, the arresting officer, friends, family, and many other folks. As Judge Reese reviewed the facts of my case, it became clear that I had been subjected to a bad public defender at my trial and did not deserve to be locked up.

Judge Reese looked out at the courtroom with a grandfatherly warmth and compassion. "Now here's a young man that shouldn't have done nary a day in jail." (Much love to you, Judge Reese. God bless you.)

His words were as sweet as angels singing to me. He commuted my sentence and said I could go home on probation. My files would be sent to Pensacola, so I didn't have to travel back and forth to Montgomery to check in with my probation officer. Before, my momma would visit me whenever possible with my baby brother and baby sister in tow in a mess of tears. Now she had tears of joy. I was coming home!

So learn from me. Watch who you keep company with. Find good friends and keep them close. Treating people right will always come back to bless you. It's a simple trade-off, but it doesn't cost anything to be nice to people. It will always come back to bless you.

10. I'm Coming Home

ONE OF THOSE friends who had written on my behalf was none other than my boy, my brother, Roy Jones, Jr. Once I got back in town, I picked up some work, first at Mom's Buffet, then selling clothing with an outfit called Mo Money. Eventually Airborne Express became my day-to-day job to pay the bills. Every chance I got, though, Roy and I would go ball.

Roy and I were like long-lost brothers. In between trials when I was back home, Roy picked me up to go play ball, and I wondered, what kind of music does he like? It's kind of hard to get into a rhythm if you're listening to something with no beat. I'm partial to old-school rap and my favorite band of all time, New Edition.

Well, I got in Roy's jeep, he cranked up the stereo and what should come out but English American rapper, Slick Rick.

Aw yeah. I figured Roy and me were gonna be good.

Roy kept up his daily routine of jumping rope, shadow boxing, hitting the heavy bag, and working out. But he never missed basketball. That's how much he loved it. It would shock people to know he could run two or three hours on the basketball court and then fight—and win!—a match the very same night. His stamina had no equal.

Roy liked having me around. He was raised to be a competitor and to fight everyone, but with me, he found a brother and a supporter. We would ball two to three times a day, and his love of the game equaled mine. Friendship with Roy also meant hanging out at the gym to watch him box. The very first time he invited me to the gym for a sparring session was another special moment.

Roy was faster than lightning. I watched him catch a former world champion with a jab to the body, and then in a moment, fake a jab and throw a left hook. I was highly impressed.

Riding back home, I said to Roy, "Man, what you did in the sparring session—faking the jab and throwing the hook—that was sharp."

Jones looked up, surprised. "Big, you saw that?"

"Yeah, you jabbed him to the stomach and then faked

a jab to the stomach and caught him with a left hook."

"Huh," Roy remarked. He stared off like he was thinking about something.

The next day at the gym, Roy faked a jab and threw a right hand while sparring. I was in awe of his speed and flexibility. I hadn't yet realized that my gift to just pick up and internalize sports was allowing me to pick up on details that few first-timers could recognize. The same gift that showed up in my youth and made me a natural at basketball, football, and baseball had transferred to boxing.

On the ride home, Roy turned to me. "Yo Big, what'd you see today?"

"Man, you faked even me out this time. Yesterday, you faked a jab and threw a left hook, and today you faked to the body and threw a straight right hand."

At the time, I did not know what my observation meant to Roy. Most people with his kind of special, generational talent pick up "friends" easily. Oftentimes, those so-called "friends" only want a free ride and a meal ticket. I was not only having a good time with Roy; I cared about him and his craft. I was paying attention, and I loved to watch him work. Plus, I saw details others would miss if they didn't care or weren't paying attention.

Next day, I received a phone call from Stanley Levin, Roy's advisor. Stanley asked me to come sign a document for one hundred dollars. In Roy's generosity, my car needed a battery, and he was quick to help me out.

But then Stanley said something else. "Roy has instructed us to put you on the payroll."

I couldn't believe it. "What? Why? I mean . . ."

"Look, Roy likes you and wants you on the team."

He didn't have to tell me twice. Work in sports with one of my best friends? That was a no-brainer. I wasn't seeking to impress Roy. I was just being myself and being a friend. Here was a trade-off that paid off in ways I could not have imagined.

Roy and Stanley had planned a trip to Disney World and invited me along—just another example of Roy's generosity. Our time together whether on the court, in the ring, or just hanging out allowed us to trade knowledge and skills, sharpening one another.

However, my invitation to the gym came with a warning. Big Roy had a reputation of intimidating those coming to see his son. Roy told me to just hold my ground against Big Roy. He was like a mighty guard dog trying to protect his family. If he smelled fear or thought something wasn't right, you were in for it. Armed with this knowledge, I stood my ground, showed Big Roy the same respect I would anyone else, and we coexisted just fine.

At nights, Roy and I had the gym to ourselves. We would engage in shooting, dribbling, passing, rebounding, and defensive drills. Roy had the mechanics mostly down pat, although today we both have to laugh about his shooting style back then. He had at least three different ways he would shoot the ball, a recipe for inconsistency and inaccuracy. I called it to his attention, but pretty soon he'd be back to switching up his shot.

Finally, I couldn't take it. "Do not change your shot another #$%@ time!"

Roy got the point.

We were both teachers. As I trained him in the mechanics of basketball, he taught me the mechanics of boxing. A lot of wannabes in basketball think anybody can just pick up a ball, dribble, and shoot. Even with my natural ability, I had to train to excel. Same with boxing. The simplest thing can be done wrong and ingrain poor skills.

My assignment with Roy was to hold training mitts or be the "mitt man." If you're the mitt man and you don't do the job right, your boxer won't get the maximum potential out of his workout. You have to be ready to catch a jab, catch a right hand, a left hook, or an uppercut, but still maintain distance while allowing the boxer to punch all the way through. Sharp reflexes are a must, and bad habits would limit the fighter's effectiveness. I was more than happy to accept my role.

Shortly after that, Roy and I started playing in the city basketball league. We were good. We traveled from town to town, destroying all other teams. Roy began to realize that if he had applied the same dedication to basketball as he had to boxing when he was young, he could have played professionally. Likely he would have. He is the definition of a winner.

After one notable victory, Roy said, "Big, if you and I would have met earlier in life, I would have been the basketball player, and you would have been the boxer."

Well, I'm glad things turned out the way they did. Roy is a credit to his hometown of Pensacola and home State of Florida. Having become a world champion many times over, Pensacola is in the house!

Roy Jones Junior became my absolute best friend in the early nineties as he charted a meteoric rise in boxing, starting off as unstoppable and undefeated. I was able to enjoy the fruits of his labor with him, yet our friendship had nothing to do with his fame or what he could do for me financially. We genuinely loved each other as brothers and always had each other's backs.

My association with Roy led me to another friendship that would mean more than I could ever realize. While we continued our tour of dominance, we were called in to scrimmage with the Woodham High basketball team, whose head coach was now none other than Benny Washington, the older brother of Glenn. I always thought Benny didn't like me, but that wasn't it. The truth was, Benny had wanted me on his team, and since I played for a rival team, he was being careful. As I said before, Benny was a no-nonsense coach who taught and inspired discipline and loved competition.

Benny showed me there was no ill will toward me by taking things a step further. He invited me to be a shooting coach at his basketball camps. I loved working with kids! Benny would go on to coach my little brother Vonsha who was born to Momma when I was seventeen.

Coach Benny was funny. Knowing I have a classic knockdown shot, he really liked to mess with the kids who thought they were hot stuff. Today I'm a little older and honestly . . . a little heavier (LOL). He would bait and switch a cocky kid. He'd point to me and say to a kid,

"Hey, look at that old guy. He's kinda fat, ain't he? I bet you can't beat him shooting."

The kid would take the bet confidently but end up either upset or in awe because I never lose a shootout! Benny became a wonderful friend and close confidant to this day. Times would pass where we needed to rely on each other. I'm so glad to count on him in my corner.

Again, in a world where people let pettiness rule their actions, neither Benny nor I took our past battles onto the court. We moved beyond whatever supposed tension there was between us, and we have become family. That's an important trade-off, pettiness for loyal friendship. Live that way, and you'll never lose.

11. Best Man

I **CONTINUED WORKING** with Roy in the gym as his mitt man. He headed out of town for one match, and as he had not yet achieved the peak of his fame, the match was not televised. I had no way of knowing what the outcome would be, and it was eating me up. Later in the evening, my mother called me to the phone. It was Roy telling me that he won.

I was super excited for him, but at the same time, I expressed regret about not being able to be there. Like a true friend, he replied, "Don't worry. You won't miss too many more." That proved true. After that night, I only ever missed a couple of fights through his illustrious career due to other obligations.

Roy's passion for basketball continued, and we won the city championship that year. Riding high on that success, the city of Pensacola buzzed because his next match was slated for the Pensacola Civic Center. We got right to training in order make sure he maintained his undefeated record.

Being in my twenties and full of energy, I prided myself on being in my best shape just like Roy did. I determined to jog with the champ each morning, side by side, sweating it out together. Soon I learned that our definitions of the word jogging were not even close! Roy was running a marathon out there! I don't think he had ever heard the word quit, and if he did, he couldn't define it or spell it. The man was a machine!

I learned pretty quickly that I would have to ride a bicycle just to keep up. I swear he was trying to kill me. This type of jogging was something strictly for boxers.

To make weight on the day of the weigh-in, Roy needed to shed another pound or two, so he would have to make one final run before that. I woke him up at five that morning but realized we were having one of our brutal Florida storms with thunder and lightning. I thought, well, I guess that's it for the run, and went back to bed.

Roy, on the other hand, was truly dedicated to his craft. He crystallized my understanding of what a trade-off really is. Rain or no rain, lightening or no lightening he was gonna get his jog in. Forty-five minutes later, he returned to my room dripping wet, ready for the weigh-in.

On our way to the scales, Roy told me he had prayed for the lightening to stop until he completed his run. As if in a vision, he saw the clouds part, and a little early morning light broke through. He thanked God for listening to him and finished his run. Once his run was completed, the thunder and lightning resumed.

Roy made weight and went on to win the fight in convincing style.

Later that night, we went out to dinner and returned to his parent's house. Something his mother said from that night always stuck with me. She gave me the kind of warm motherly look every person loves to see. With big brown eyes, she smiled and said, "Don't you ever leave my son."

I never did. Roy and I are still the best of friends today. Not a day goes by where we don't talk on the phone to each other. He is my brother and close friend.

I never could figure what Mrs. Jones saw in me that wasn't in the rest of the friends hanging around Roy. A dear friend of mine, Pastor Eddie Frey, thought it only right we contact her to discover the answer for this book. Here's the interview.

Pastor Fray: What did you see in Alfy that caused you to say what you said to him that night?

Mrs. Carol Jones: Alfy was different. He was not like all the other guys hanging around my son. He genuinely cared for Roy. I knew he loved Roy and would be a positive influence in his life. I believe within my heart that Alfy would always tell my son the truth.

Pastor Fray: Are you proud of your son's legendary career?

Mrs. Carol Jones: Like all mothers, I am proud of my son. I would not have chosen that profession for him, but that was his choice. That is what he wanted to do, and I gave him my blessing.

Mrs. Jones's belief in me remains comforting to this day. She saw in me what I tried to live out: being a true friend, a brother, a father, an assistant—whatever was needed for those around me. When an opportunity came to befriend Roy, it wasn't out of selfishness, but just in trying to live as I was taught. Before meeting Roy, I had no real love or interest in boxing. It wasn't even on my radar. But to support a friend, I took up a new skill.

We will not be allowed to fully orchestrate the direction our life will take. As Martin Luther King, Jr. said, sometimes one's life pursuits and fate are determined by one greater than oneself. Either way, I ended up with the valuable trade-off I had prayed for back in that cell just a few years earlier. I did not choose boxing. I chose a friend, and boxing chose me.

12. Boys to Men

THIS WAS A special time in my life. I was thankful and appreciative that Roy chose me to share these experiences with him. A week before my first scheduled trip with the champ, the two of us made a trip to the University of West Florida to play some basketball where they were having a three-on-three tournament. Before we could even locate a third player, Roy and I joined the tournament. We spotted a random player and asked him to come play with us. There was certainly no hesitation on his end. At that point, it didn't matter who we picked, we could take on any third person and make a championship team.

The tournament winners would receive a pair of tennis shoes each. You must be kidding; the great Roy Jones playing for a pair of tennis shoes? It ain't no lie! Roy was a real competitor. He played, and when he played, he played to win. It must have shocked everyone that we finished as the tournament winners. Evidently, the tournament sponsors got together and decided that Roy did not need another pair of tennis shoes, because here we are twenty-plus years later, and we have not received those free shoes.

Some of you may be thinking that the opposing players would give Roy a pass on the court or play him soft. Rest assured that was not the case. Rather, they wanted to dispel his athletic greatness. Still, as a boxer and as a basketball player, Roy had phenomenal skills that were untouched.

My very first trip with Roy was a memorable one. We headed to Great Gorge Ski Resort in New Jersey. It was time for fight prep. In camp with the champ was Ray Mercier, Charles Murray, and Alfred "Ice" Cole.

After arriving, Roy and I learned that the resort had a full basketball court. Forget all the preliminaries and fight prep. We changed clothes and made a beeline for it.

My shooting touch was in rare form. From all over the court and well behind the three-point line, I was lighting it up. I wasn't counting, but I believe I hit almost twenty-three points before missing a single bucket.

The very next morning, one of the guys witnessing

this amazing feat woke up trainer Alton Merkerson—whom we called "Coach Merk"—and asked him, "Who is that guy that Roy has with him?"

Ha! I was still known to shock and amaze!

At the same time, Roy looked out for me. Based on superficial appearances, standing at an average height of five feet, ten inches, I didn't look like I could ball like I do. I won quite a few friendly bets. Roy, having experience dealing with a lot of tough characters, warned me to be careful not to do that too much because I might look like a hustler. He was a true brother who looked out for me just as I tried to look out for him.

Most of the training for this fight was done during the day and we jogged or ran at night. Roy wore all white while he ran to stay safe. I did not make the first night of jogging, but I was ready for a good run the second night. Still, I could barely keep up with Roy and keep him in sight.

When we got back, Coach Merk and Hank Johnson were inside of their condo finishing the meal, an exacting diet to keep the champ's body finely tuned. Ray Mercier was waiting to dine with us and thought he would mess with the heads of a couple of young bloods.

Ray gave Roy a deathly serious stare, square in his eye.

"Man be careful out in them woods. There are bears, and there's an old [American] Indian hanging around this camp."

It seems the bear and the Indian were working together. The bear would attack you, and the old Indian would beat you up and throw your battered body back down the hill.

True or not, I wasn't taking any chances. I hadn't seen bears in Pensacola, and I wasn't about to meet one now! So, when we went jogging the next night, I killed myself to keep up with Roy! I could barely see his white jogging suit, but the adrenaline must have kept me close enough. When Roy placed his key into the lock that night, I was right beside him.

Hey, I had to protect the champ.

Okay, I was scared. Are you happy? I said it! Oh, well. Better safe than sorry.

After a week of training and eating all the right foods, I had had enough. I was sick of eating nothing but health foods and was ready for some junk. At first, I did not know how to express my urge to the champ. Remember, he's the boxer. His body is a well-oiled machine. Mine, not so much. But I had to say something.

So, away I went, hoping it wouldn't upset him. As we

rode around town, I pleaded my case. "Roy, man, I cannot handle another healthy food meal. I am sick of all this 'good' eating."

His response to me was, "Exactly." (This is how I know Roy is my brother.)

I was pleasantly surprised, and we were off to Burger King for some junk food.

Look, if you can't enjoy your trade-offs at some point, then why make them?

One health food I would never touch was apple juice. Of course, juice was a staple for an elite athlete like Roy. It never appealed to me, so to keep from drinking it, I would always say I was "allergic." But like I said earlier, Roy's definition of jogging is equal to marathon. We came in from one of his grueling jogs, and I was dying of thirst. There was nothing in the refrigerator to drink but apple juice.

Impulsively, I grabbed a bottle and started chugging.

Roy, aware of my "allergies," rushed over to save me. "Big, I thought you were allergic to apple juice!"

If you'd seen me caught telling a story that day, you would have seen a Black man blush. I had to come up with something quick. I said, "Naw, it's cucumber juice."

Ha! I was just that thirsty. Turns out I didn't hate apple juice after all, and yes, I have been drinking apple juice ever since that day.

In 1992, Roy had a huge fight night in Atlantic City at the Taj Mahal. Roy Jones vs Percy Harris glowed on the marquee. To many, the boxing match was the main event, but the boxing match itself was a breeze. Roy easily dismantled his opponent that night.

However, the big surprise for the camp was Roy's choice of ring music. The song was by New Edition. (Did I mention they're my all-time favorite group?) The message behind the song, "Boys to Men," did not go unnoticed by me. After that fight, we were on to bigger and better things. Fight after fight, I watched Roy's greatness unfold before the world. I was ready to ride along with him. Life was also about to bring some bigger things and some bitter things.

13. Dream Girl

LIFE WITH ROY was great, but life was going to get even better. I was riding high. Roy had sold me the red Jeep he owned. I converted it, put in crushed velvet, and painted it burgundy and gold. On the back were the words "Big Al." Man, I was fly! I'm telling you!

As much as we loved traveling to spots like Vegas, New York, and Atlantic City, Roy and I both love our hometown. Sometimes we would even miss flights on purpose because we didn't want to leave. Still, even with all the excitement and fun of travel, I was missing something. I needed a woman who felt like home, a beautiful soul with which to rest myself.

I don't feel the need to tell you all my exploits of loves gained and lost. Each relationship had its pleasure, and each had its pain. Through them, I gained six beautiful daughters and a son who are all still my pride and joy, and that gives me no regrets.

But I needed something more, and one night, I found my soul mate.

A group of friends and I went out like any other weekend for a good time of partying and dancing. The music was loud, and the women were fine as can be. Once me and my boys were done, a group of us stopped over at the Krystal Burger across the way from the club to grab something to eat. As we stood outside around our cars, I was just being me, telling stories like I do, and I had everybody laughing.

If you know me, you'll know I always had a thing for Vivica A. Fox. I've watched this beautiful Black woman's career and always admired her beauty, charm, and talent. I said if I ever had a chance that I'd shoot my shot. Now, here in the midst of us chilling and laughing was a fine woman who looked just like her, I mean, just like her. While I'm shooting the breeze with my friends, this honey is laughing the hardest.

People tell me that I look like Cedric the Entertainer. I must have some of his funny bone. As we all stood around, you know how people just kind of find their way next to each other somehow, just through that natural magnetism? Suddenly we were next to each other, and she was laughing at everything I said.

Doubling over laughing, she put her hand on my shoulder and leaned into me. I caught a whiff of her. Man, even after a night of dancing, the fine ones still smell good! (You know what I'm saying?) Something happened right there. At that moment, we just bonded. The energy passed between us or something. I don't know how to explain it. If you've ever been in love, I mean really in love, you know what I mean.

I was helplessly in love.

From that time on, I was with Felecia Katrice Johnson—"Fee Fee"— and she was my ride or die for real. She was my support in everything. As my bond with her grew tighter, my confidence in Roy and his success was bringing us the greatest success. Roy, being my brother, loved Felecia like a sister, and he loved all my family like they were his. It was nothing for him to give her a call and check up on her as a brother does.

One time, we were on a trip in Vegas. As the undefeated lightweight champ, the money rolled in freely for Roy now. Some people might have seen that as an opportunity and thought one about taking advantage. But Roy was my friend, my brother. If he took me in his confidence or asked me to take care of something, you can be sure I was gonna do my best.

Roy motioned to an envelope full of hundreds. Since anything could happen in a big city like Vegas, Roy said to me, "If anything happens, this is bond money for both of us." I nodded, and we went about having our good time.

As we partied, I was in and out of Roy's room never giving the money a second thought. Some hangers-on would have grabbed a spare hundred thinking, "Roy's rich. He won't miss it." But the thought never crossed my mind.

As the trip came to a close, Roy grabbed his envelope and checked what was in it. He saw that not one cent was missing. It wasn't even touched. I think even he was amazed that I didn't feel entitled to take a little taste for myself. Roy had to tell Fee Fee.

"Fee! Man, I ain't ever gotta worry about Big stealing from me. Every time I give him something, it never comes up short!"

What a friend to be bragging on me to my girl. Roy didn't have to do that, but that's how loyal he is. It made me proud to know that by just being myself, Roy had that confidence in me. I could only think of both of our mothers in that instance: my mother for teaching that lesson of honesty so many years before as she did at work, and Roy's mother for telling me to always stay by her son because I would look out for him.

14. That's the Way We're Livin'

I HAVE TO dedicate a chapter to some heroes and greats who I admire. Excuse me if I name drop, but hey, don't tell me all of y'all picked this book up because you just saw me on the cover. I know you want to hear about Roy and some of the stars! Plus, these are some of the great payoffs of my trade-offs.

I seem to always have gotten along with the celebrities when I was with Roy because I've gotta be real with them and treat them like regular people. I have to tell you about one experience with the GOAT—the greatest player of all time—Michael Jordan.

Sometime during the second three-peat of the Bulls in the last half of the nineties, I got to meet Mike in the flesh. I knew I would get the chance because Roy Jones was the first boxer to sign the Jordon brand. We went to a commercial premiere party for the brand.

Mario, a co-worker, waited in the lobby. And who would walk in next but Michael Jordan himself! Mario spoke to Michael and said, "What's up, Mike? This is Big Al."

Michael smiled and said, "What's good? Nice to meet you."

Mario jumped in and said, "Hey, Alfy take a picture with Michael."

To my shock and amazement, Michael said, "Yeah, let's get a picture."

As we posed for the picture, I whispered to Mike, "You know how everybody is talking about who is the next Michael Jordan."

He said, "Yeah, what's up?"

I said, "You are taking a picture with him right now."

Mike chuckled and patted my stomach. "Yeah . . . twenty pounds ago."

We left for the big office where a lot of the known celebrities were hanging. Roy sat by the door, and Mike started to chat Roy up. It was awe-inspiring to see two legends just conversing.

Mike turned around and patted my stomach again and told Roy, "Your boy said he is the next Michael Jordan. I told him maybe twenty pounds ago."

Roy got a serious look on his face. "Mike, he can shoot for real."

To get that kind of validation, even after some years with my friend, you can imagine my head probably swelled so big I wasn't gonna be able to get out the door.

I walked across the room to chill against the wall. I look to my left and the person standing next to me was Michael Jordan. I had to tell Mike the story of when my mother heard me curse when he was a freshman and he dunked on those three players from Wake Forest.

Impressed with the fact that I remembered not the typical highlights, but was a real fan of the game, he said, "For real, man?"

I said, "No disrespect to him, but just like you dunked on Patrick Ewing under the goal waving his hands." Then I told Mike how Roy and I studied his game and how he used to attack the double team. "I used to imitate your shots, but I couldn't do all of that high jumping."

Mike seemed genuinely interested to talk shop. But I had to let him know, "Mike, you my dawg, but we could never play together."

"Why's that, Big Al?"

"Well, Mike, you like that ball and I like that ball! We both can't have that ball in our hands."

Mike couldn't hold in his laughter. Good times!

I had the chance to hang with another basketball hero of mine. Some years later at an event, I met none other than Julius "Dr. J" Erving. We were able to chat and get a photo together. I had to rib him a bit.

"You a bad man, Doc, but Roy and me could beat you and Maurice Cheeks right now."

Doc looked at me in disbelief. "Man," he said, "I'll dunk on you in my church shoes!"

I backed off with that!

Roy helped me refine my skills from being just a beginner in the boxing world to becoming a true technician and coach in my own right. I even got to meet the legendary Muhammad Ali.

I worked with a variety of fighters, and please indulge me as I name them here now: Charles Whittaker, Gabe Brown, Lemuel Nelson, Derrick "Smoke" Gainer, Isaac Salter, Ezra Sellers (R.I.P), Vernie Torres, Frank Wood, Kippy Warren, Victor McKinnis, Ike Quartey, David Izonritei, James Walton, Arthur Williams, Vince Phillips, Kareem Ali, Saben Cura, Jason & Keon Papillion, Carmelo Colley, Donald Clark, Keith Mullings (R.I.P.), Nate Campbell, and Alfred "Ice" Cole (who starred in Ali alongside Will Smith). Them's all my boys!

My first pro fight working by myself as a coach led to another impressive encounter. I know I sound like a broken record, but much appreciation to Roy for allowing me to spread my wings and expand out into areas without a hint of jealousy or worry.

In 1996, ESPN2 showcased their first-ever boxing match. Regrettably, we took the L, and this being my first fight, it was a slight blow to my confidence. I headed to Jacksonville for Roy's next fight. As I got off the elevator, who should I bump into but legendary boxing judge and analyst Harold Lederman and legend George Foreman in the flesh. I had no reason for them to notice me, but they were both very friendly, true to their reputations. Harold told me, "Alfy, you looked better than your fighter on TV. If he had listened to your instructions during the fight, he would have won." George Foreman agreed.

Wow! Confirmation from two legends in the boxing world. I was determined to keep up my training.

Here's a takeaway I have to repeat: You're going to take some Ls. Unlike that first time I picked up a ball as an eight-year-old kid, not every first outing is going to be a smashing success. But if you gain a new passion, keep at it, and give it your best. Success isn't necessarily in the win, but in the effort you give.

15. Is This the End?

TRADE-OFFS IN LIFE are not always by choice. Some are unavoidable. And run as much as you can, you cannot hide from your enemies. I still had to learn how to face the greatest enemy head-on.

Because of my association with Roy, I was known as the success in my family. In the community, I continued to volunteer where I could and mentor young men to have a good life and not make the mistakes I had. When not working with Roy, I was a driver with Airborne Express.

Living the lessons Daddy, Grandmomma, Momma, aunts, uncles, and coaches had taught me had led me to what was practically paradise. With Felecia by my side and standing in Roy's corner, nothing could stop me. Roy continued his unstoppable rise in the world of boxing. The wins just kept coming. And unlike certain other boxers, he was afraid of no one.

The wins kept rolling off. Twenty-five–zero. Twenty-six–zero. Twenty-seven–zero. Thirty–zero. He was sure to do the unthinkable and maybe even get to fifty–zero one day. But we weren't worried about that. One fight at a time. Though we were men, we were young men, living faster and faster, high on success. As I've said, I don't need to rely on drugs or drink to be fulfilled. The thrill and glory of sport and the love and affection of friends and family can give you all you need if you just let it.

In the midst of this, I could always turn to Daddy (Granddaddy Ulysses) for wisdom. He was a steady guiding hand with wise words when I was at a loss. And I couldn't be prouder than to know that Daddy was proud of me. When we got together, he would just look at me and smile. That smile would fill my heart. Just another big heart that ran in the family.

Age was starting to catch up with Daddy though. He took his time to share whatever nuggets of advice when he could. Early in 1994, Roy and I dropped in to visit with him. Again, I have to restate that the great Roy Jones was riding with me to visit my granddaddy. As great as he was, he took to time to see my family.

Daddy had this gray in his eyes. It was like a gathering

storm far on the horizon. We greeted him and sat with him for a bit. There was a pause in conversation. Daddy gave me this slow, long look and then stared off into the distance. Then he said, "Boys, let me tell you something. Whenever you can, get you some land. People can always build more buildings, but they can't make any more land."

We sat with that for a second. Daddy was trying to prepare us for something, something deeper, and we knew it, but we didn't want to consider any further meaning behind it. Daddy also let me know that he needed to talk to my momma and uncle because he had some things he needed to share with them in person. I assured him I would let Momma know. She had every intention of getting with Daddy as soon as they could all make the time.

After chatting a little while longer, we said our good-byes. As Roy and I drove away, we couldn't help but have tears in our eyes at seeing this proud man, who had done so much for his family, struggle through the pain of aging.

A few weeks later, Daddy asked me to take him to the drug store. We got in my fresh Jeep with the top down in the warm Florida sun. Daddy was just smiling, and I felt his pride shining on me more than the sun in the sky. Everything is all right, I thought.

But on April 15th, the day before my thirtieth birthday, I received news that no one wants to hear. My cousin Jarvado called me up. He had actually lived with Momma and me for a few years as he finished high school, so we got pretty close. But the call I got that day was devastating.

Jarvado: Hey Big.

Me: Yo, what's up? (I could tell from his shattered tone that something was up, and it wasn't good.)

Jarvado: Big, you got a minute?

Me: Yeah, what's going on?

Jarvado: It's Granddaddy. He . . . he died.

For the first time in forever, I was totally speechless. Everything around me became a blur, and I felt pressure in my chest. The only father I had ever known was gone. Coming up on thirty years and riding success, I felt really like a full-grown man, ready to take on the world. Now I sat like a little child, lost and alone.

I tried to get a hold of Momma, but she was at her favorite pastime, bingo. We didn't have cell phones then, so I would have to wait until she got home. I sat on her front porch. Despite humid spring heat, I was cold and numb.

When Momma finally pulled up and approached the

house, I just didn't have it in me to be anything more than to the point. "Momma, Daddy's gone."

She looked like she lost half of her soul in that moment. Life just drained out of her as she stopped and could only say, "Not my daddy. Not my daddy." The grief was too much to express.

At least we had each other.

The next few days passed in a gray fog, that same fog I experienced when my father passed twenty-five years earlier. This time, though, I was in the middle of it all and understood everything that was going on. We pulled together as a family, and one by one, got ready the arrangements for the wake. My cousin Omar in Dallas worked in a funeral home and showed me how they prepped the body. He left me alone with Daddy's body for a few minutes so I could talk to him. I was amazed at how at rest he looked, like he could just sit up and talk to me right then. It almost seemed like old times as I just expressed my love and thanks for all he did for Momma and me.

Here I was, thirty, a full-grown man. I had to be strong for the family. But when we got to the wake, the reality hit me. Like a flood, the tears just poured. Warm streams flowed down my face, and I couldn't put two words together. Momma was a complete mess, and the rest of the family was overcome with grief too. As we were gathered together, a warm hand rested on my shoulder.

Coach Merk, a man who taught me so much while working with Roy, stood there feeling my pain. He was a mason like Daddy, there in brotherly support for us.

"Al, how are you, son?

"Hey, Coach. I just . . . I wasn't ready for this."

"Look, I know it's hard. Death is never easy. But remember that you're the success and pride of this family. They all look at you and look to you. If they see you down, everybody else will be down too. If you're strong, they can be strong."

I gathered myself and put on a determined face. Yeah, Daddy was gone, but the family was looking to me to be a pillar of strength, and they would need me more than ever now that he was gone. I felt I could take that knowledge and now be ready for anything once again.

I received another unexpected reward for the trade-offs of working hard, continuing to stay out of trouble, and supporting the family wherever I could. At the wake, one of Daddy's mason brothers came up to me with a box. It had some of Daddy's mason things in it.

He said, "Your granddaddy was proud of you, and he wanted you to have this."

This was a sacred trust from Daddy from beyond the grave. I took it and nodded. When I got home, I put it in the top of my closet without looking inside because I know masons take their society seriously. When my Uncle Ulysses Junior became a mason, I dutifully gave it to him, still not knowing what was inside. It could have been a million dollars for all I knew. I just wanted to respect Daddy and honor him the best I saw fit.

I tried to stay strong. Death would continue to be a presence in my life, just like it is for everyone. I had to brace myself like a man and be strong for everyone. I knew these things in my head, but the reality of that had not gotten fully into my heart yet. It's hard enough to lose someone older who has a full life to look back on. But nothing can prepare you for losing someone young.

I was only beginning to be prepared to learn how to face the greatest enemy.

16. Heart Break

THE PRIDE OF youth makes us think we're invincible. At times, it even allows us to push beyond our limits. On top of the world, Roy had decided to move up in weight class from super middleweight to light heavyweight. His reign of domination could not be contained!

No true athlete attempts any feat without his eye on the ultimate prize, and Roy moved up by keeping his eye on gaining the belt in a third weight class. Only the rare few have ever tasted such glorious heights.

One after another, the opponents fell, but in 1997, the unthinkable happened.

Changing classes brings with it new challenges, but the fundamentals of being great never change. Roy was a natural at his sport, and a gift of God-given athleticism was developed through supreme work ethic and dedication to his craft. I may seem biased—okay, I know I'm biased, but you can't convince me that Roy was not the best boxer alive. No one could touch him, especially not Montell Griffin.

Griffin faced Roy in Atlantic City and proved to be a capable opponent. He got a quick lead on Roy, but by round nine, Roy, as usual, had figured out his opponent's tricks and was leading by all accounts. Sometimes while inside the ring, Roy and I would engage in a full conversation.

Roy said to me, "The commissioner and the referee are up to something." He felt it, he sensed it, he knew it, and he was right.

In the confusion and speed of the match, Griffin realized he was outmatched and took a knee. Roy was so caught up in the furor that he didn't realize his opponent was down, and he landed a right-left with blazing speed. Griffin slumped to the floor with a dull thud and was counted out.

Victory! But wait . . .

The ref announced that Jones was disqualified for an illegal blow.

What? We all were visibly stunned. In a moment, dreams of 50–0 were gone. This felt like South Korea all over again. First, the referee's instructions were to always protect yourself. Second, the referee was out of position to properly make that call. Third, if Montell Griffin would have risen and knocked Roy out, that same referee would have said the fighters are instructed to always protect themselves.

With this, I was hurting inside; according to a family member who was watching at home, the expression on my face brought tears to the eyes of those present. Disqualifying Roy was ludicrous! But it happened, and there was nothing that to be done about it.

Roy was not a dirty fighter, anything but! Before and even after the Montell fight, if Roy was clearly outclassing or getting the best of his opponent, he would motion for the referee to intervene or stop the fight.

For example, his passionate heart was evident in the Vinny Paz fight. Although Vinny had been medically cleared to compete in the match after recovering from a neck injury he got in a car crash, Jones was conflicted about hitting him in the head, especially the neck area.

During this time, I was still in awe of whom I was working for. This realization manifested itself in the James Toney fight. While in the dressing room, Roy began sharing his fight plan with me. You did not hear me. I said Roy shared his fight plan with me, Alfy Smith.

Wow!

After the Montell Griffin disappointment, we re-grouped. The sting of that blemish lessened with time and in many ways only made us hungrier for success. Roy regained his title some short months later. In the ring or the court, we were total beasts.

With the sting of my grandfather's death fading into the background, I faced the future with greater hope. The embodiment of that hope came in the form of my little brother, Vonsha. Like my mentors before me, I had always tried to be a big brother to those who wanted to come under my wing. But at seventeen when my mother told me I was going to be a big brother to a flesh and blood little brother, I had an untouchable pride.

Vonsha became my shadow when I was around. He was determined to ball like me and admired me as any little brother would admire an older brother. He was gifted in his own right, and I nurtured every gift in him I saw. I poured brotherly and even fatherly love into him. He was warm and big-hearted like Granddaddy, Daddy, and Momma.

Like I said, big hearts run in my family.

My life was on a high. On February 14th, 1998, I performed the greatest gesture of devotion I could for the love of my life. Fee and I got married. A fine romance it was. I knew I was the man now. She was and always proved to be my best friend. We never went to bed angry with each other, and my children never heard us argue. We were in lockstep as partners, and nothing could stop me! I was on top of the world.

But I was about to experience the depths of darkness.

On March 4, just over two weeks after Fee and I got married, I was visiting with Momma and Vonsha, who was thirteen years old by then. Something wasn't right with my baby brother. I sat on the porch watching the kids play basketball, but instead of playing with them, Vonsha just came out and sat with me. When I got up and went inside, he followed me in. He was shadowing me everywhere, even more than usual.

I decided to go visit a friend in the neighborhood, and Vonsha came along. I told him about a vivid dream I'd just had, that Granddaddy had died in my arms. Without knowing it, I had been crying in my sleep all through the night.

The heaviness I was sensing about Vonsha gathered like a grey cloud in his eyes. He gave me a slow look and said, "Big, are you afraid to die?"

"Naw," I casually replied. "Death is a part of life. Death

comes for everyone, and when it's our time, it's our time."

"I am," Vonsha said blankly.

He sat still for a moment, but to this day, that moment felt like forever. The cold stillness in his eyes penetrated me to my core with a look I had never seen before. His pupils were wide and black, like he'd seen a ghost.

I shifted uncomfortably.

Silence again. Anyone who knows me knows I'm lighthearted and have to break that tension. I tossed off some casual comment, but the tension held. He just kept still, staring like he was experiencing something super-natural.

As the night went on, the temperature got a lot colder than normal for March. Unnaturally cold. Nights dropped to just above freezing, not good for Florida blood. At least it kept the bugs away. As the night passed, I tried to shake the feeling that something was off, but the bone-chilling wind whistling through the trees created an ungodly emptiness in me. I held Fee extra close.

The next day, I didn't have any work and was at home chilling, which wasn't normal for me. Usually, I would go play ball or something, but for whatever reason, I just stayed home with Fee. Out of the blue, the phone rings, and it's my sister in a fountain of tears.

"Alfy, Vonsha passed out at school, and he ain't responding."

Fee and I went into a panic. We could not get a hold of Momma, who was playing bingo, so we called Eleanor, Fee's momma to tell her what had happened. She was with Fee's young nephew, Tameric, who was just four or five years old at the time.

She later called us back and said, "Tameric told me Uncle Vonsha's dead."

Her words shot through me like a bullet. Of course, Tameric couldn't know. How could he? Still, the thought was too much to consider.

We pulled up to Woodham High to find an ambulance right outside. I ran to the ambulance door, but they wouldn't let me in.

"That's my baby brother!" I cried.

"Okay, sir. Just follow us to the hospital."

I jumped back in the car with Fee, and we rode the bumper of the ambulance all the way to Sacred Heart. But something wasn't right. We covered a little more than two blocks when I blurted out to Fee, "My brother's dead."

Fee tried to be positive. "No. Don't say that, baby."

But I just knew. When they've got a chance to save

you, they rush. But they weren't rushing now, and the truth seemed inevitable.

When we got to the hospital, they let me into a room to sit with him. I held his hand as he lay there so still and peaceful. Finally, a doctor came in and made it official.

March 5th, 1998, Vonsha Blow was no longer with us.

I just held my brother, weeping uncontrollably. Like the true brother he is, Roy and his team were there. The hospital room was full of people, friends and family. The sobs in the room rose from barely audible to deafening.

I lost my baby brother that day.

The doctors said it was an enlarged heart that took him. It was the size of a grapefruit.

Like I said, big hearts run in the family.

Nothing can prepare you to lose a child or a young sibling. Everything I had hoped for him was gone: The championships, the graduations, the games, the cook-outs, the wedding, anniversaries, the celebrations . . .

I became a shell of myself for some time. Up to that point, I had lived my thirty-two years for basketball. If you didn't know where to find me, all you had to do was check a court in Pensacola. But for days after Vonsha died, I couldn't touch a ball. Days turned into weeks and weeks to months. Fee tried to console me, but I found no comfort. I mean, in the very place where I was my greatest self, where I felt the fullness of my soul—on the court—that's where my baby brother died!

Prayers were difficult. At times, I couldn't eat right. I could only listen to music, mostly sad songs, but even the fun songs would bring me to tears. Through it all, Fee was a support and a rock. I cannot overstate how valuable that woman was to me in those times. If you've found a good wife, you have a treasure. And she was worth more to me than gold.

If I was bad off, then I can't even begin to describe Momma. She would just sit and watch the VHS tape of the funeral and cry.

"Don't do that, Momma," I would gently say. But she would never stop mourning him. To bury a thirteen-year-old is a pain that you can never recover from. If she lost half of her soul when Daddy died, she lost the other half when Vonsha left us.

Somehow, I knew she would never truly be at peace until she was with them.

As I mentioned, Benny Washington and I had become tight. Benny was Vonsha's coach and he was at the high school state finals when he got the phone call that Vonsha had collapsed. Benny is what you might call a man's man, tough and determined, yet he was the one who helped me pull through. I learned that those young teenage boys on Vonsha's team hadn't been too proud to cry at the sight of him passed out on the floor that day, blood pouring from his head.

I knew I had to be strong for the rest of the family. We were coping step by step.

At the same time as Benny was offering consolation to me, death suddenly struck again. Just two months later, in May, Benny's dear wife collapsed. She was his partner for over three decades. Three weeks later, she too lost her battle, leaving Benny and his two sons without their rock. Death was a ruthless sniper taking out our most cherished loved ones without warning. The whole sports program of Woodham and the community struggled. But we found a way to drag ourselves out of the quicksand together.

I should stop and share a lesson here. I never thought I would get over the grief of losing Vonsha, but to do so is just another trade-off, bigger than so many others. Trade grief for joy. Trade death for life. Trade selfishness for brotherhood. If I didn't have those loved ones to lean on as I grieved—Benny, Roy, and my dear Fee—I don't know what I would have done. The love Benny had showed me paid off by me being there for Benny and his family when they needed support. We got through it together, and that's a priceless thing.

But like I said before, those unexpected deaths were a terrible weight on our communities. The Woodham basketball program struggled. I thought I would never pick up a basketball again. Through the pain, I poured myself back into the world of boxing.

Still more challenges lay ahead.

17. Been So Long

IT WAS 1999, and a new millennium waited on the horizon. It turned our attention to a reason for hope, but it didn't stop time and unexpected events from wreaking havoc on us.

While driving for Airborne Express, I flipped my van and came near to death myself. Thankfully, however, I walked away with minimal damage. Just before I was about to work the corner for a boxing match in Biloxi, Momma stopped by for a visit. I told her about flipping my van the day before and thanking God to be alive.

Momma looked at me real slow through gray eyes as if something just hit her. Then she gave me directives for reorganizing her affairs. She wanted me to take the lead, of course. As my sister was in a "wild child" phase, Momma wanted her excluded. I objected but she eventually prevailed. I hated to think what looking after Momma's affairs would do to my baby sister, and we don't want to leave things like that undone when we go.

I didn't know then that Momma and Grandmomma were not close when Momma was growing up. Grandmomma had even treated her quite poorly. You would think I would have picked up on it, but Momma didn't let on. I only found that out later after various family tragedies and losses had Grandmomma ask Momma for her forgiveness, and they began to patch up old wounds. Believe it. It's never too late to set things right with those you love.

Well, the weight of love and loss in Momma's heart must have been too much to bear. She carried losing my daddy, her daddy, and Vonsha only the year before. She had carried the tension between her and Grandmomma for years, and though it finally resolved, the strain had to have affected her. Yes, Momma had a big heart, and it was a heart attack that got her late that Saturday night when she returned home from a trip to New Orleans with Stepmomma.

I received a call Sunday morning that my mother was gravely ill. I rushed to the hospital, intent on seeing her recovering. Instead, I heard the worst thing imaginable. My momma, my nurturer, my lifeline, had passed away.

I was distraught. I can only thank God for Felecia by

my side, helping me as I made the funeral arrangements. Nothing really gets you ready for having to approve the body of your mother for the viewing. She was too young, only fifty years old. But like I said, I knew she'd never be at rest until she was with Daddy, Granddaddy, and Vonsha. Now she was finally at peace.

Momma's death was deeply unsettling for me. It just further impressed upon me that the inevitable strike of death can come at any time. Just as darkness inescapably rules a certain portion of the day, we must accept the darkness in our lives. But darkness will always trade off to light at some point. We lean on those close to us and find the invisible will to move on.

This brought me to a point in my life where I needed to do more with myself and my community. I had been working with Airborne Express for a while and was ready for something different. Boxer Smoke Gainer, one of Pensacola's own, had started a charter school named in honor of his grandmother, Ruby Gainer.

Billy "The Kid" Lewis, another of Pensacola's finest, knew they needed a behavior tech and coach at the school. It gave me a chance to put my education and skills to work. I interviewed for the job and was immediately accepted.

But I had not touched a basketball since losing my

baby brother over a year earlier. Would I still have my touch? Could I lead these young men?

I need not have worried because once God blesses you with something so deep, getting back in is like getting back on a bicycle. Once we passed a probationary season to start our team, we were always successful. We got to the playoffs in the first year, and I never had a losing season. One school we always beat was Escambia Charter, our local rivals. With a good family and fast friends, I was still a winner.

The takeaway: Grief will come, but it can't kill the heart of a winner. You can only have the heart of a winner if you have people to help you grow that heart. At some point, we have to move on. This is a trade-off we need to make to get all we can out of life and most importantly, help others.

If I had tried to ball just for myself, I would have had no joy in it. Taking those kids under my wing gave me reason to enjoy the game again. I was able to pick up somehow and go on. I would have to. Fee needed me. The kids needed me. Roy needed me. As a family, we pushed ahead knowing it wouldn't be the last death we would face.

I would have to be ready to let them lean on me as I had on them.

18. With You All the Way

A FIGHTER'S WEIGHT must not exceed the imposed fighting limit to qualify for his class. Fighting in a different weight classes is challenging for any boxer, but Roy has the rare distinction of being champion in five different weight classes: middleweight, super middleweight, light heavyweight, cruiserweight, and heavyweight.

But sometimes along the way to becoming champions, we can make decisions that lead us to a heartbreaking L. Regardless, we can still make trade-offs in ways that result in ultimate victory.

For the first Jones vs. Tarver fight, Roy had to come down in weight after winning the heavyweight championship against John Ruiz. Tarver started talking trash about Roy. That got under Roy's skin, so he instructed his managers to make the fight. In hindsight, maybe not the best thing to move so quickly, but pride gets the best of all of us, and every great champion has had to learn to overcome it, Jordan, Kobe, LeBron, and even the impeccable Roy Jones Jr.

To come down from heavyweight to light heavy, Roy punished his body. As one of the commentators for that fight, George Foreman said that Jones was fighting totally on heart. And he was. Roy's body was in shock. The weight loss zapped his strength. Tarver had a good showing, but despite the physical challenges, Roy was the clear winner of Jones vs. Tarver I.

But in the second fight, Tarver got the victory. He caught Jones with a lucky punch, and in boxing, one punch can change everything. Within or outside of ring, RJJ is not one for making excuses, so the public didn't know that Roy was dehydrated during the fight. Because he was low on the body's most essential element, water, the night belonged to Antonio Tarver.

This was a rude awakening for the whole team. We all have to face the reality that we're not invincible. And even if we seem to be, nobody stays at the top forever. That's why they say, remember where you come from. If you step on people on your way up, you'll meet them all again on the way down. Better to have true friends at your side to carry you through the lows.

Well, Roy has never forgotten where he came from, and I'm proud to have been a friend who could see the facts and offer some encouragement even in the rare loss. Even the HBO announcers had to acknowledge that Roy was heading back to the dressing room with supporters and friends, most of whom had been with him through his entire pro career. I'm glad to count myself as one.

The HBO cameraman followed us back to the dressing room after the Tarver fight, where Roy got hugs and warm appreciation from his dear friends. Even in defeat, Roy received heaps of praise from announcers. He handled defeat like a man and made no excuses. I was glad for people to see the character of a true champion.

The camera happened to catch a quiet moment between me and Roy. I just had to speak from my heart. Roy had been unstoppable for so long, and anyone who was going to face him would have to be scared. Roy had already handled Tarver once, and I knew Tarver had come with that fear. I sat quietly by Roy who was looking down, processing what just happened. I said to him, "A scared man is a dangerous man."

Roy's head popped up like a fire had lit under him. "That's right!"

Team members started chiming along realizing that ultimate truth. "Yeah, he was scared!" some chimed in. We were down but not out.

What is the takeaway?

The character of a man is not defined by his victories, rather the character of a man is defined by how he handles losing.

It is my strong belief, that if RJJ had never fought as a heavyweight, he would have retired as an undefeated fighter. Roy Jones, Jr.'s boxing career was on display for the entire world to see and judge. History will record him as one the greatest prizefighters to have ever lived. His blistering speed and ring IQ were second to none.

I may be biased, but surely Roy in his prime would have beaten several boxing legends in their prime. Like Ali, Jordan, and Tiger Woods, generational greatness lived in Roy Jones Jr.

After becoming his head trainer, Roy and I won five straight fights. Concerning his boxing career, I was not there in the beginning, but I was there to the very end. From the bottom of my heart, I once again would like to thank RJJ for believing in me as a trainer and friend.

19. Who Do You Trust?

A FEW YEARS after we lost Vonsha, Fee and I found ourselves opening our home to a wonderful treasure that helped fill the hole in my heart. In 2003, my baby sister had a baby boy. She was young at the time and not equipped to care for a family, so we agreed to raise her son. His name? Vonsha Blow, just like his uncle, my baby brother. We took him in from the time he was two weeks old.

Fee was the rock of our family in all this. While I was the face and success of the family, she was always there making sure Vonsha got to his games. She always had dinner ready when I got home and made sure the kids kept up with their schoolwork. She was a warm mother for the girls too.

My baby girl Jada is a real daddy's girl. Whenever I would get home, she would get my things, take my shoes and rub my feet. She would want to fix my plate and serve me. Fee would have to run her off sometimes!

"That's my husband, Jada!" We would have to laugh. Man, we were tight.

I continued to reap the benefits of supporting Roy as I continued to meet notable figures and stars. One year we attended the Celebrity All-Star Game. I got to sit and watch the game with Jamie Foxx, who I had come to know in recent years and would talk with. I mean, he would call my house! From the moment I met him, I could tell he was serious about his music. I had no idea that I was again meeting another person of immense greatness as he would go on to star in the movie Ray and win the Oscar for Best Actor. Yet, even after all that success, here we were, just a couple of fellows chatting it up.

Now, who should be the coach of one of the celebrity All-Star teams than my TV crush, Vivica A Fox! I always said that if I were to meet her, I had a whole speech memorized. Well, I guess that night I was more like mesmerized. Me and Jamie started messing around.

I joked, "Hey man, go over there and get me Vivica's number."

Jamie shot back, "Man, what, you scared?"

Well, after the game was over, who should walk toward us but Vivica herself! I don't know if Roy or Jamie or somebody put a bug in her ear to mess with me, but she came right over and asked me, "Hey, what are y'all doing later?"

My mouth dropped, and my body froze. Speech was out the window! So much for shooting my shot.

That same weekend I got to meet WNBA stars, Rebecca Lobo and Lisa Leslie. I couldn't resist trying to playfully flirt with them. They both had the same response: I was too short.

The year 2005 brought a catastrophe to our beautiful Gulf area. The nation will never forget the sudden impact of Hurricane Katrina that caused over eighteen hundred deaths and $125 billion in damage in late August that year. We did all we could to step into action to help the community, no matter who it was.

As most folks already know, New Orleans was hit with the worst of it. That city is only three hours from here. If you were to hear me and Roy training back then, we might have had on songs of rappers from No Limit Records, Master P's label. (Later, I even got to ride with Mystikal in a limo once and asked him about one of his songs that my fighter Jason Papillion could not figure out. Right there he rapped the verse and showed me how he flipped it, and he could flip it well.) Well, all those folks are based out of New Orleans. Mr. Magic, one of their rappers, ended up signing to Roy's label, Body Head. We had hung out and were very friendly.

After the storm, I spotted Magic in Home Depot. We saw each other, dapped it up, and checked on how each other was doing after the storm.

"Man, Big Al," he said, "it hit my family hard. I brought everybody this way, and they're staying with me here. I got some of them looking for work. If you know of anything, can you help us out?"

I felt his pain, and I didn't hesitate. "Come by the house tomorrow, and I'll see what we can do."

We hugged and headed back to getting what we needed to fix our homes up after the storm.

Magic brought his cousins by the next day, and I took them to the track where I had some friends who I thought might be able to help. All four of them got jobs. I was just happy to help.

Now that I was working at the school, it gave me another opportunity to try and bless people. Kids would sometimes throw lunches away without touching them. Before they could toss them out, I would grab what I could and give them to folks I knew in need. (For example, one poor fellow came by the gym regularly when Roy was sparring. I tried to help him out. When they found him dead one day, there were over a hundred lunch trays in his apartment.)

From the day Magic let me know about his family troubles, I would drop off a stack of lunches at the house where his family was staying. I would just make the trip, leave them in the garage, and head on my way.

The third or fourth day I did this, Magic's momma was sitting in the garage. When she saw me coming up with the lunches, she started crying. She looked up at me, eyes full of tears, and said, "You a child of God. Ever since we got here, you've helped us. You've done got four people jobs and come by here every day with food."

I wasn't looking for praise. I just didn't think to do anything else but help. I'm so glad Daddy and Momma, all my family taught us how to be family to everyone in need. Just hearing Magic's momma say those kind words was enough payoff for me.

I must put others ahead of my own interests. That is the biggest trade-off I've learned in life, and it always finds some way to pay off. Cousin David says I will help others to the detriment of myself. But what else do you have to live for other than those you love the most?

One day, Sylvester Stallone called, wondering if Roy

would play his opponent in his final Rocky film, Rocky Balboa. Once again, Roy, ever loyal and humble asked me what I thought. Again, do you hear me? Roy Jones, Jr. wanted to know what I thought he should do!

I took a second before replying. "Well, that movie is only gonna pay you one time. They want you to get up to two hundred pounds for it. The quick change in weight to take the role will put your body in shock again. You're better off taking more fights, and you'll come out with more money that way."

And Roy took my advice! He could see I was looking out for him, not my own interests. Somebody else who didn't care about him would tell him to go ahead and get wrapped up in Hollywood and then try to get their own place in the film. But I didn't care about that. I wanted what I thought was best for my friend.

We got hit again with death and defeat shortly after that. Roy and I were doing all we could to support local communities. Our favorite way to do that was, of course, charity basketball games. And you know I had a chance to show out every time. I was proud to be able to even do one for Coach Sellers' school, Georgia State University.

In July 2007, Roy and I were in Biloxi training for media for the upcoming fight with Anthony Hanshaw.

Roy, his twins, and I were sitting at the buffet table one morning when I got a cell phone call from Derek Roberts. I figured it was for the upcoming charity game in Monroeville where I would get to see my old buddy Lloyd Patrick again. I picked up the phone and immediately started to rib him. "Boy, I know Lloyd's just hunting you down."

Derek said, "Yeah, Big Al, you sitting down?"

I said, "Yeah, man."

Derek said, "Man, they found Lloyd dead this morning at the hotel."

My enemy struck again. I lost it right there. Roy did his best to offer some consolation, and I finally pulled myself together. I hated to think about this reality, but I soldiered on. The only thing to do was to keep leaning on each other and give the world our best. Above all, Fee would be there when I got home to nurture those deep wounds. To trade off the pain, I focused on Roy and our craft.

The next year, Roy agreed to fight Joe Calzaghe, and HBO did a twenty-four seven documentary on the fight. I became especially famous back home, being seen running with Roy all around New York.

We went to a Knicks game at Madison Square Garden before the match. I got to chat it up with Allan Houston and other Knicks players. Before the game, I was allowed to shoot around with the team and casually drained ten three-pointers in a row. An old man was sitting in the stands and yelled out, "They oughta dress you out tonight!"

I still had it!

Still, life was like riding a roller coaster backward. Great ups and intense downs that came unexpectedly. What else would be in store for me?

20. Rewrite the Memories

IT WOULDN'T TAKE long for life to provide more rapid ups and downs. We would soon get back to winning ways in the ring, and I was enjoying success on the court with my kids. But past demons sometimes come back to bite you. How you deal with them is once again a trade-off that can pay off for good or bad depending on what you do with it.

I wanted to be paid as a behavior tech and coach for Ruby Gainer Charter, but because of that ill-fated court case so long ago, I had two credits taken from my college record. Essentially, I had no degree. In the transfer of probation from Montgomery to Pensacola, something got missed in the transfer, and my files were never brought up to date in the system.

In 2009, situations forced Ruby Gainer Charter to close. I had to find work somewhere else, but what would

I do without my degree? We made the trip to check on my case files and get things straightened out. The clerk found it in the depths of the courthouse basement, the literal bowels of the building!

That court case in Montgomery was my only trouble on file. I had caused no other problems. I had to comment to the clerk. "I told the guards and everyone that they would never see me in there again, and they ain't ever seen me in here again. Ever!"

With that cleared up, getting my coaching certificate was a matter of nine hundred dollars. Well, lo and behold, who should want me to coach at their school other than Mr. Jerome Chisolm, head of Escambia Charter who I was undefeated against! He even paid the nine-hundred dollars for me to get my certificate so I could coach and get paid accordingly! Once again, I would be going to a rival, and it would be to their gain. I kept them in winning seasons for the next six years.

This forced trade-off from one school to another was another blessing in disguise. Mr. Chisholm became another wise father figure. An intelligent man with a firm but warm demeanor, he was and is greatly respected by many in our community. He taught me the value of making sure I present myself in a way that gains others' respect. You only get to make one first impression.

They didn't just gain a solid coach in me, but a fierce supporter in Fee Fee. She would be the loudest spectator on the sidelines, yelling at referees. Man, she got into it so much that one game, the ref threw her out. She was the nicest person in the world until that ball went up in the air!

Well, once she got thrown out, Mr. Chisholm sat there praying, please don't let anybody say anything to her on the way out so she doesn't go off. Fee marched to the door. You could see the steam coming off her as she stomped away. She got to the exit, turned around, and said, "And all y'all can kiss my . . ." you know what! That's my baby. Ride or die for sure!

Fee was always there, keeping my head up through the loss of Daddy, Vonsha, and Momma. She was even with me as Grandmomma's light faded.

Grandmomma and I always stayed close. In 2011, her advanced age finally caught up with her. She could be at peace knowing she had resolved the strained relationship she had with my momma. Grandmomma was a strong woman, and when she told me the story about their troubles, it was the first time I had ever seen her cry.

I told you before how Grandmomma was always my

biggest supporter. She always singled me out and told everyone about my games or when I was in the paper or on TV. She would be in the stands screaming and cheering as I played. And without exception, every year in March she would call up the whole family. "Don't forget that Alfy's birthday is coming up on April 16th," she would remind them.

Me and Fee were going every Sunday to see her and bring her a Sprite. Fee had actually worked in a nursing home before and was familiar with caring for folks in their final stages. We were visiting Grandmomma one Sunday with Uncle Junior and Auntie Candy when Fee got up and suddenly went to the lobby.

I went after to check on her. She had tears in her eyes.

I asked, "Baby, what's wrong?"

Her experience in the nursing home came back to her. She sighed. "Baby, I see death in your grandmomma's eyes."

I hugged her and offered reassurances and made my way back to Grandmomma's room. Grandmomma was only barely lucid. She saw me and said to everyone, "Yeah, Alfy's got a birthday coming up on April the 19th."

Uncle Junior looked at me and whisper, "Hey, homes. It's over. She's never got your birthday wrong."

She passed the following Thursday, March 24, 2011. And here I was going through that routine again. It was not easy, but I was becoming a little more numb to death as it had visited so many times. My saving grace was always Fee. She was there for them all.

The year 2013 was especially hard. Fee helped me find my uncle's grave when he passed. She was there with me when Mr. Magic, the rapper who I had kept in touch with and helped out during Katrina died in a horrible car accident on the way to a show. And she was my rock when my boxer Ezra Sellers died unexpectedly in 2013. He was taken by heart problems. (I seem to attract people with big hearts who can't handle the strain.)

But nothing, nothing, nothing could prepare me for what soon happened. There are trade-offs we don't want to make, trade-offs life forces on us. If I thought I had faced storms before, I was about to go into the eye of the hurricane and barely make it out alive.

21. Since I Don't Have You

I WAS ALWAYS gaining good friends who became like family. My fighters and friends Nate Campbell and Jason Papillion were real brothers. These men had keys to my house, could go to my house while my wife was home by herself, and I had no jealousy or suspicions whatsoever.

Nate saw Fee as a big sister, and they even became pedicure partners! (Sorry Nate!) I love Nate and Jason, and we had always had a good time together. They were just more to add to the family.

As I tell you my next story, I want to preface it with this trade-off. You have got to trade your pride for humility and always show love. Let bygones be bygones and never let a day go by without telling people you love how you feel for them. You never know when you might lose them, as I had already seen at this point in my life. But that enemy death will cut you where it can the deepest.

March 15, 2015.

On that day, the breath literally left my body, and I thought I lost my whole reason for existing. It was a trade-off that taught me much and am still learning, but I tell you, whatever it would take to not have made that trade-off, if I could go back and change it, nothing in this world could stop me from altering history.

My family and I hosted Jason Papillion and his family one evening. Fee prepared a wonderful dinner, and we were all having a great time. Before we sat down to eat, I leisurely walked outside to find my wife sitting in her favorite chair on the front porch, staring out. Something was on her mind. Something was bothering her, and she had a gray stare in her eyes. She gave me a slow, serious look but then smiled, and went back inside the house.

She opened the screen door because she was feeling hot. As she walked towards the kitchen, I gave her a loving poke. She said, "Not now, baby," but gave me a big smile. She ambled in and got things ready.

After that filling meal, we continued chatting and laughing. Before long, it was time to escort our guests to their vehicles. They headed outside, and we exchanged warm goodbyes.

We stood together on the lawn, enjoying the cooling

spring breeze. We discussed purchasing some new furniture and walked back into the house, arms around each other's waists. It was a beautiful feeling. It was home.

Worn out, Fee lay down on the love seat with our goddaughter, Twinkie. I stepped outside to hang out with some boys whom I was mentoring. Time passed, and I realized our daughter Jada needed to be picked up from work. Fee was originally going to do it, but I could tell she was wiped out from entertaining. I came in the house to see her laying there with Twinkie, and I whispered, "Fee, I'm fitting to go pick up Jada."

She said, "Thank you, baby," and I headed out.

Thank you, baby. Three little words that mean so much to me now and still ring in my head.

I went to get my little sweetheart, Jada, from her job at Firehouse Subs. I saw longtime friend Michael Lee and greeted him. Just then my cell phone rang. It was my daughter Nakia. She was a wreck, crying, and sputtering out broken phrases.

"Daddy!" she wept. "We found Momma outside on the porch, and she ain't responding." I felt the blood drain from my face. Jada jumped in the car and knew something was wrong. I didn't say a word. I just silently sped home to make sure my wife was okay.

We pulled into the driveway, and I felt an eerie still-ness. I don't know how to describe it. It was like the air just stopped. It was chaos and stillness at the same time. There Fee was, laying on the ground by the chair where I would usually sit.

My neighbor from across the street hovered over Fee, trying to revive her. Time stood still, and I rushed over to my baby. I grabbed her arm. It was cold. It didn't feel human.

I gently whispered, "Fee Fee . . ." Her head dropped, and bubbles came out of her mouth. "Oh, God! No! NO! NOOO!" My voice roared in pain. My mind raced like a gale wind. On my knees, holding her close to my chest, I begged God, "Please, heal her. Save her! Save her! Please, God. Don't take my wife."

I cried frantically. Just moments ago, she was so full of life. She's just sick. She's just having a stroke or some-thing. She's gonna be okay. I know it. I know it. I couldn't suppress the unimaginable feeling inside me. I felt the unthinkable, but I hung onto hope.

That same cursed blur happened all over again, all still, yet all chaos. Flashing lights. Men jumping out of an am-bulance. Fee on a stretcher. Questions fired. Confusion.

My head ached. I paced around the yard, facing the

sky. God, please! Please don't take my wife. Please don't take my wife. Clutching my chest, I felt my shirt, wet and clinging to me.

Then Fee was in the ambulance.

I looked at the EMT. "Please tell me my wife ain't gone."

He was a young man. Still, a trained professional. He knew he couldn't take my hope away now. He wasn't authorized to pronounce anything, let alone . . . that. He put his head down.

Fee was rushed to the hospital, and the family gathered, all of us, waiting, full of pure anxiety. It was me, my girls, Twinkie's father, and Roy and his wife. I looked at the clock. I had never seen a clock move so slowly. Hurry up, dammit!

I prayed harder. Please, God. Don't let my baby leave me. Please don't take my baby from me now! Then I pleaded with her spirit. Baby, don't leave me now. I need you. We have so much more to live for, together. Not like this. Not like this. God no. God no. No. No. No! No . . .

Finally, a doctor approached. His face had no color. He looked like a man who had just finished running a marathon with nothing left in the tank.

"Who's Alfy Smith?" he asked flatly.

"Me," I replied, hanging onto the hope that he'd tell us everything was gonna be okay.

The doctor choked out his words. "I'm sorry. We've done all that we could do. We lost her."

My daughters collapsed to the ground with an ungodly outburst that must have shaken the whole floor. I looked around at everyone else in vain, as if maybe they had some other answer, like somehow, they were going to make this not be true. Roy's wife broke down crying, and Roy had tears in his eyes.

Just like that. It couldn't be. But that was it. She was gone.

That day, food lost its taste. Nature lost its beauty. Every song played a sour note. My everything, my forever, had changed. I had lost my wife, my best buddy, the mother of my children, my lover, my greatest supporter, my ride or die, my reason for existing. Felicia Katrice Johnson-Smith was no longer a part of this world.

I wailed, and anyone who was still trying to hold back broke down too.

I must be dreaming. This isn't real. This isn't real. Somebody wake me up now! God, why? Why, why, why, why, why?

I didn't know what to do. Fee had been so full of life. I was fragile, and the wrong thing could have turned me into a crazed man.

Roy kindly said, "Bro, if my wife was in there with all them wires and machines hooked up to her . . . Don't go in there and see her like that."

Somehow, that was the right thing to hear. There's no way I could have taken the weight of that sight.

And what took my baby?

It was her heart. Always the heart.

The community surrounded me with love and support, but it was of little use. I sank into a depression I had never known before. Even with all the losses I had experienced before—my father, my granddaddy, my baby brother, my uncle, my momma, my grandmomma, friends—nothing had prepared me for this. I was depressed past the point of death.

In the days following my greatest loss, I would have gladly welcomed death. Life had totally lost its meaning. Work, basketball, even family or how I would be remembered—it meant nothing.

To approve my granddaddy's, then my momma's, and now my wife's body for the funeral—I don't know how I did it. Well, I know now. It wasn't me at that moment. If family and friends hadn't carried me, there was no way I would even be alive today.

My dear Pastor Eddie Frey was a man I resisted knowing at first, but he became a friend and mentor. I call him "Jesus' best friend." His words of guidance were invaluable to me throughout the ordeal and after. He pointed me to Psalm 23, the famous psalm that says, "The Lord is my shepherd; I shall not want."

Who else was by my side during all this? Nate Campbell, Fee's "little brother," was right there for me. He got to me as fast as possible. I had never worn an outfit that wasn't the sharpest I could find, but for my wife's funeral, I could barely put myself together. Nate came in and made sure I was dressed like I was meeting royalty to see my wife off, and he was right. She was my queen, and she deserved my best.

Billy Lewis and Jason Papillion physically carried me into the funeral. I was a man without a spirit. At the funeral, when asked to speak, I got up not knowing what to say. My heart was empty, yet full of pain. I had nothing prepared. But then the words started pouring. I let everyone know that you've got to tell people how you feel about them every day. Don't let the chance slip away to send someone your love. If you have something against someone, resolve it. Life's too short, and resentment is not worth holding onto. If you can't be at peace with your brother or sister, if you've got malice in your heart, how are you gonna meet Jesus with a clean conscience? My words just tumbled out in a flood of emotion, and there wasn't a dry eye to be seen.

After the funeral, I was told my words had even out-done the preacher that time. Reverend Fray said on a scale of one to five, I was a six. People who hadn't talked since high school came together on that day. I found out afterward that a lady who had worked with my wife went home after the funeral and called her sister whom she hadn't talked to for ten years.

Somehow, without knowing it, I was able to use my deepest pain to help bring people together.

The funeral line went on for blocks and blocks. It felt like the whole town came out to see Fee off. Somebody commented it was bigger than Johnnie Taylor's funeral in Dallas.

And who else was there with me in all this? Who was a friend? Who was there when he didn't have to be, a man bigger than all of us, the pride of Pensacola and world champion extraordinaire?

Roy Jones, Jr.

The morning of the funeral, I didn't think I could make it out. Roy had a simple and profound way to help me see that she was better off than us. He sat with me and just said, "Big, you gotta think of it like this. It'd be like if you hit the lotto, and your neighbor don't want you to go live better."

It just clicked with me. I had to let her go. I didn't want to, but I had to let her go.

That's not to say I recovered at all in the days to follow. I would go into my room after work and lay in bed in the dark. My daughters would come in and beg me, "Daddy, you need to get out of the house." It was hard to hear, but I knew they were right.

For the first time ever, I needed to start drinking a little something to ease the pain. I'm not endorsing it, and I'm glad to say I never became dependent, but everything was upside-down. What did anything matter anymore? If I hadn't been supported enough, I would have willingly drunk myself to death.

Each day, I floated through the land of the living like a wandering spirit with no resting place. All too soon the school year was over, and there wouldn't even be that to distract me from the pain.

Faithful friends rallied around, and each one provided a brick for me to piece my emotional house back together. Folks like Roger McDuffie and Clarence Ward warmly came up to me and said, "Coach, you're gonna be all right."

When the last day of school arrived and all the teachers had left, I stayed in my office cleaning up. There wasn't anything left to clean, but I was finding any reason to avoid going home. Mr. Chisholm, head of the school, mentor to me, and a dear friend, walked in. He paused for a second and just looked at me. My eyes were stone cold, trying to hold the water back.

With that strong, warm wisdom and such depth of life experience, Mr. Chisholm looked me straight in the eye. "I know what you're doing, Alfy, but you gotta go home and face it."

That was just enough to push me through. I wasn't facing reality head-on. This would be the first summer in two decades that the trips and fun planned for Fee and me would not include her beautiful smile, her warm embrace, and her tender words. I was still struggling to cope.

With Fee, I never had a losing season as a coach. Since I lost her, I haven't had a winning season. It's been a slow process. But I make it one day at a time. Whenever I hear "I'm Coming Home" or "Helplessly in Love" by New Edition, I weep. Finally, I started to find some comfort in music again.

It's hard to believe that my life meant I got to be a close friend to my boy, Ronnie DeVoe. Ronnie always calls and gets me backstage passes whenever he's performing in the area. Once again, here is how blessed I am in life. He's an R&B legend, and he takes time out for me!

At the Funk Fest in Mobile, I got to see Ronnie as he was performing with Bell Biv DeVoe. At a previous show, they had taken a picture with Fee. I was so proud of that and kept a blown-up copy. Before the show, we took a picture together holding that photo, and they even signed the print of them with her. Such real brothers. You can see the pain in their eyes for the hurt of losing my wife. I had to be strong because they were about to go on stage, but I am eternally grateful to them for taking time for me.

Not too long after that, still reeling from loss, I called Ronnie looking for some comfort. I'll never forget his words, "Big Al, I just bought some movie tickets, but if you need to talk, I'll throw them away." That let me know he was a true friend.

How in the world did I get to be friends with another one of my heroes?

My daughters knew about the picture with Bell Biv DeVoe but never paid attention to what was written there.

One day, I asked Jada to record me doing a TikTok singing "I Do Need You" by Bell Biv DeVoe for Fee. I gazed at the picture, just swimming in my imagination that she was there. Jada looked at the picture and saw that Ronnie and Bel Div DeVoe had written, "I Do Need You."

Jada burst into tears, and so did I.

Let me just thank here and now New Edition for all the joy and warmth they've brought into my life. They helped save me in my darkest hours.

The biggest trade-offs in life come in moments like these. If you want to be worth something and be able to give to others, you have to make trade-offs. You have to trade:

Pain for comfort;

Isolation for support and friendship;

Wasted time for useful hobbies;

Wallowing in pity for taking care of yourself;

Laying in darkness for walking in light;

Selfishness for giving;

Drawing inside yourself for giving out gifts;

Cursing life for embracing faith.

It seems fitting to end this chapter with song lyrics that mean so much to me, a playlist that I hope touches your soul as much as it does mine.

To view original videos to some of these songs, visit my YouTube channel: www.bit.ly/LifeofBigAlYouTube.

"Missing You" [1]

You know I'm missing you!!

Since you've been gone

Missing you!!

Life is not the same

Missing You

Y-O-U you!

We all have had loved ones to go on and take their rest

We all have fun memories of the life that you've lived

But you know I'm missing you!!

Since you've been gone

Missing you!!

Life is not the same

Missing you!!

Y-O-U-you!

Missing you!!

We all were made sadden when the news came that you
were gone

We all look forward to seeing you in glory land

---

1   Written by Eddie Frey, performed by Katrina Washington, produced by
Anthony Williams

But right now I'm

Missing you

Since you've been gone

Missing you!!

Life is not the same

Missing you!!

I'm missing you

Missing you!!

I'm missing you

Missing you!!

Missing you on your birthday, holidays

Somebody listening

Just like me, got a loved one gone on

Missing you!

"See You In The Next Lifetime" [2]

I'ma see you when I make it home

It's been kinda rough since you been gone

Oooh

But I'm steady holding on

Since you been gone

I ain't gone front

It's been kinda hard baby

---

2   Written, performed and produced by Andre Harris (aka Flight Gang)

Up in the sky

I see ya face

When I look to the stars baby

You my guardian angel

I thank the Lord that he made you

To have you in my I'm thankful

For The time we spent I'm grateful

Girl, I miss

I just wanna kiss you

I just wanna hug you

And let you know how much I really love you

15 of March the day my life changed

Ain't been the same since that day

When the times be getting hard I gotta bow my head
   and pray

But I gotta keep on going

For our kids I make a way

I'ma see you Once again

And baby girl until that day

Been in so much pain

I ain't gone never ever be the same

You was my umbrella

Kept me dry through all the rain

Been tryna keep it together

Bump that Pac to keep me sane

Love you with all of my heart

You kept my life together

Now it's just falling apart

You was that light that shined so bright in a world that
so dark

Gotta get back to it

I can't fold

Know that this is just a test

What was the purpose I don't know

But I never Question GOD

Even tho I got a few

Wish he would have to my life that day

Baby instead of you.

"I Don't Wanna be Alone" (for Felicia) [3]

A hundred times, I don't know why

Picked up the telephone

Started to call you then hung up

Realizing that you're gone

The way I'm feeling in my mind girl since you went away

Is getting worse and worse with each and every passing day

---

3   Written and performed by Chris White of the group T'sha and Kevin Wilson (aka Kebo, also with T'sha). Produced by Timmy Fingers.

Can't understand why you were taken up away from me
Now everywhere I look your face is all that I can see
The twenty-twenty vision that I'm having now is clear
I wish this pain would disappear
'Cause

CHORUS

I don't wanna be alone no more
I want it to be like it was before
Back you were here and love was sure girl I don't wanna
    be alone
I don't wanna be alone it's true
Every thought I have girl is of you
It's so hard to carry on
Every day since you've been gone
I don't wanna be alone.

VERSE

Can someone you tell me why on earth you ever had to
    leave
And tell me now what can I do to bring you back to me
All this confusion that I'm dealing with has got to go
I don't know how much longer I can take this really
    though.
My loneliness is all the company I seem to keep

That company is turning seconds, minutes into weeks
Now years that you've been gone away seem like eternity
I wish this pain would set me free
Girl

CHORUS

I don't wanna be alone no more
I want it to be like it was before
Back you were here and love was sure girl I don't wanna
   be alone
I don't wanna be alone it's true
Every thought I have girl is of you
It's so hard to carry on
Every day since you've been gone
I don't wanna be alone.

VERSE

The other day I thought I saw you driving in your car
It seems to be that everywhere I look girl there you are
I close my eyes and go to sleep I hear you call my name.
When I wake up, I hear you too it's never gonna change.
I never thought that I could hurt the way I'm hurting now
I never thought that you would be taken away somehow.
One thing is sure in spite of things I'll never comprehend.
My love for you will never end.

Life is full of challenges, regardless of your race or background, regardless if you're rich or poor. You're going to have setbacks and dark days, but you can overcome them with the grace of God and the music and people in your heart. Life is full of trade-offs. Use them. Hang in there. You can and will overcome the darkness.

22. Try Again

THE ONE THING I love more than basketball is all my people. Even when I didn't feel it, I was wrapped up in their love and they carried through my darkest hours. To trade away the hurt, I would have to learn to give again.

Uncle (Ulysses) Junior had the same confidence in me as his namesake, Granddaddy. He had let me know that if anything happened to him, he wanted me to raise his son, Ulysses III. The day came when we lost Uncle Junior. At first, Ulysses III stayed with an uncle nearby, but the year after Fee died, when he was twelve years old, I took him in and raised him as my own. I consider him as if he were my own son, and he was a blessing.

One day at a time, I've pulled myself together. With my loving children and faithful friends keeping an eye on me, I continued to work as a coach at Escambia Charter until it ran its course and had to close. I then went on to work as an assistant basketball coach with Ms. Joanna Johannes, founder of Lighthouse Private Christian Academy. My son Vonsha played there and just graduated on May 17th, 2021. He always wore the number fifty in whatever sport he played in honor of my momma who passed when she was only fifty years old. My brother Vonsha also wore the number fifty.

I'm proud to say I have a warm relationship with all the kids I run into. Kids don't warm up to everyone, but it's been noted that they all talk to and smile at Coach Alfy. Ms. Joanna always brags on me and tries to tell the kids, "You don't know, but we have a celebrity working with us here." It's always nice to be appreciated by such good people.

I pour myself into service at the school. Anything anyone ever needs, I try to fill in, driving a bus, handing out lunches, whatever I can do to help out. I feel like God put us here to help others, and I still carry that with me. I was deeply honored to be given various awards in recognition of my service there. Ms. Joanna calls me her "angel in the hat" because I never lost that love of wearing hats that my daddy gave me when I was just a little boy.

I traded off living a life for myself to living a life for

ALFY SMITH | 165

others. Being able to focus on other people has helped carry me through after the most devastating losses of my life.

I had to chance to do that again just recently. In 2020, Hurricane Sandy hit the panhandle hard. She punched a hole in the roof of my house, and like so many others who had urgent repairs, I wanted to get it fixed.

Annie Perez, a young girl new to Lighthouse Private Christian Academy, was one of many kids who became like family to me. She always calls me "Uncle Alfy." The storm made her family's home unlivable, and they needed to get to Milton about an hour away where they could stay in a hotel and not just a shelter.

I couldn't bear to see them struggling and drove them to Milton with my last little bit of gas. When we got there, I waited to make sure they got into their room safe. As I got ready to say goodbye, Annie's grandma looked up at me and broke out crying. "Here you are worried about us," she said, "and you've got a big old hole in your house."

My heart was touched. I hugged them goodbye and headed home.

I've continued to have run-ins with greatness when young stars come through the area, like Michael Randolph (aka MJ) who played for FAMU; Elmo Shedarious Coward, who played for Grambling; Roy Jones, III;

Dwayne Kelley (DJ), Roy's nephew, who plays basketball for Sam Houston.

Nothing changes too much. I'm a little older and face some new struggles, but I still get all I can out of life. Yes, I've had a lot to be thankful for, and I am still being blessed by amazing encounters with outstanding folks. From a poor little Black boy in a small beach town to travels with an all-time boxing great, partying with celebrities, and raising a beautiful family, I can hardly believe myself what amazing things I've experienced. I even got a chance to be on television off and on for twenty-plus years through networks like HBO, ESPN, and ESPN2, and shows such as Friday Night Fights, and Tuesday Night Fights, or the Showtime network and The Keenen Ivory Wayans Show and Good Morning America. Sometimes people have come up and asked for my picture because seeing me is like seeing Roy.

But how did I get here? Simply put, trade-offs. Like I've already said so many times, you have to have dedication. Trade off selfishness for giving, pride for humility, death for life, anger for love.

What will you choose? That's up to you. But live for love and try to choose the right trade-offs, and I promise you—I promise you—it will always pay off.

Photos

Alfy on the cover of his middle school yearbook, 1980.

Alfy's mom, Elizabeth Williams, 1985.

Alfy performs in his high school variety show as a member of "True Edition," a band named in homage to the popular R&B group, New Edition, 1985.

While visiting Vegas for a Roy Jones Jr. fight in 1994, Alfred "Ice" Cole and Alfy get together. Cole, another Alfy trainee, played in the movie Ali with Will Smith.

Alfy's mom (center), his wife (right) and Alfy at a Roy Jones Jr. vs Thulane Malinga fight in 1995. They're holding Jones's IBF Middleweight championship belt.

From left to right: Chris White, Roy Jones, Kevin "Kebo" Wilson, and Alfy, 1995. White and Wilson were members of the band T'sha, whose lyrics for the song "I Don't Wanna be Alone" appear in chapter 21 of this book. Alfy managed Wilson's boxing career.

Alfy and Cedrick the Entertainer in Atlantic City, 1995.

After a Roy Jones Jr. fight in 1994, Dr. J and Alfy met in the locker room. "Alfy," Dr. J said, laughing, "I'll dunk on you in my church shoes."

Billy "The Kid" Lewis and Alfy in 1995. Alfy trained Lewis.

Marlon, Shawn, and Damon Wayans with Alfy after a Roy Jones Jr. fight in 1996.

Vonsha Blow, Alfy's late brother in 1998.

Alfy and Michael Jordan at Michael Jordan's "He's the Greatest" commercial premiere in 1999.

Michael Jordan, Ice Cube, and Alfy at Michael Jordan's "He's the Greatest" commercial premiere in 1999.

Alfy and Mary J. Blige at Michael Jordan's "He's the Greatest" commercial premiere in 1999.

Alfy, Roy Jones Jr., and Shemar Moore at Michael Jordan's "He's the Greatest" commercial premiere in 1999.

The late Mr. Magic and Alfy in New Orleans for Roy Jones Jr. vs Richard Hall matchup in 2000. RIP Mr. Magic. Gone too soon. (1956-2009)

Alfy and Roy Jones Jr. (center) with the "Rated PGs" (Teddy Weet, right; and Dynamite D, left) in 2000. The "Rated PGs" was one of the first music groups Alfy managed through Knock Out Productions, a now-dissolved company he shared with Roy Jones Jr.

Alfy and his late wife, Felicia Smith (1971–2015) in 2000.

Cuba Gooding, Jr. and Alfy after a 2001 Roy Jones Jr. fight in Los Angeles, California.

Jamie Foxx and Alfy at the 2003 NBA All-Star weekend
in Cleveland.

Alfy and Vivica A. Fox at the 2003 NBA All-Star
weekend in Cleveland.

Lisa Leslie and Alfy at the 2003 NBA All-Star Weekend. When Alfy tried to flirt with Lisa, she grinned and told him that he was too short.

Rebecca Lobo and Alfy at the 2003 NBA All-Star Weekend. (Like Lisa Leslie, Rebecca told Alfy that he was too short for her.)

Alfy and Emmitt Smith in 2003.

Alfy meeting Hall of Famer Bruce Smith on the set of *Pros vs. Joes.* 2003

Alfy and the entire cast of *Pros vs. Joes* in 2003.

Quarterback Randall Cunningham and Alfy hanging out after shooting Pros. Vs. Joes in 2003.

Eric Dickerson (left) and Kelvin Willis (right) with Alfy (center) after wrapping up the shooting of Pros vs. Joes for Spike TV in 2003.

Carmelo Anthony and Alfy outside the ring at a Roy Jones Jr.'s fight in 2003.

Kadeem Hardison and Alfy at the 2003 NBA Slam Dunk Contest.

Alfy and Joe Jackson, 2004.

Superbowl Champion Derrick Brooks and Alfy after one of Brooks's 2005 games with the Tampa Bay Buccaneers.

Alfy and Vonsha Blow, Alfy's nephew, in 2009. Alfy raised Vonsha like a son from the time he was just two weeks old.

Gabrielle Union and Alfy after a dance during Michael Jordan's 2010 golf tournament in the Bahamas.

Anthony Hamilton and Alfy at Michael Jordan's 2010 golf tournament in the Bahamas.

Scarface, one of Alfy's favorite rappers, and Alfy at a Roy Jones Jr. fight in 2013.

Jalen Rose and Alfy at an after party following one of Rose's games in 2013.

Former World Champion Nate Campbell and Alfy after Campbell won a 2013 fight in Destin, Florida.

Alfy and his son Jamel Jefferson, 2016.

Dan Shugart and Alfy in 2018. Shugart, of WEAR Channel 3 News, covered Alfy playing basketball, coaching basketball, and coaching boxing.

Alfy working the corner for Roy Jones Jr.'s last Pensacola fight in 2018.

Ronnie DeVoe and Alfy after one of Bell Biv Devoe's shows in 2021.

Fred Robbins signing his MN Vikings jersey for Alfy in 2021.

Alfy's daughters clockwise from top left: Nakia Smith, Tiara Hawkins, Turkesa Jefferson, Teresa Jefferson, Tyanna Smith, and Jada Smith; 2021.

Lumon May, the commissioner for Escambia County District 3 since 2012, with Alfy in 2021. May helped with the Evander Holyfield Camp.

Alfy and Faison Love in Atlanta, 2021.

Michael Randolph Jr., Southwestern Athletic Conference (SWAC) 2021 player of the year and Alfy in Tallahassee.

Gotti of "Boo and Gotti" and Alfy, 2021.

Keon Papillion, his father Jason Papillion and Alfy in 2021. Alfy had the pleasure of training both father and son.

Acknowledgements

THIS BOOK WOULDN'T be complete without giving a whole lot of thanks to my people, and I want to start by thanking legendary hall of fame boxer and nine times world champion, Roy Jones Jr.—the best to ever do it—for his support and friendship.

Much love to Pastor Eddie Frey, one of God's faithful servants.

To Indigo River Publishing for believing in me and to Don Miller without whom I could not have written this book.

Shouts out to my longtime friend Rochester Johnson Jr., better known as "Chester." I'm one of the first clients signed under his consulting firm, 324 West Consulting, which advises other celebrity athletes and entertainers. We have great plans together for the future.

Much gratitude to the recording artists who put their music out in the world and add the beat to my life. A few of them gave me permission to share their lyrics in *Trade-Off*: Eddy Frey for "Missing You," performed by Katrina Washington (Coach Benny Washington's sister) and produced by Anthony Williams; Andre Harris (aka Flight Gang) for "See You in the Next Lifetime" which he wrote, performed and produced; and Chris White of T'sha for "I Don't Wanna be Alone," a song he wrote and performed with Kevin Wilson (aka Kebo, also of T'sha), whose boxing career I managed. The song was produced by Timmy Fingers. Thank you!

A special shout out g to my partner, "Ray Ray" Russel Jr., a former radio host of 93 WBLX who passed away on April 17, 2009. I was introduced to him by my good friend Sherman Davis. I hung out with Ray Ray when I played basketball at Faulkner University and he attended Alabama State University. I had a chance to see him do his first comedy show, and he had a chance to see me promote my first comedy show, where he was the co-star. That event was RJJ's first time performing as a rapper under Knock Out Productions, Summer KO Laugh and Jam. Cedric the Entertainer headlined show and 93 WBLX promoted it.

Another shout out goes to LSU star quarterback, Jamarcus Russell. As a teenager, he played in the basketball game honoring my thirteen-year-old little brother, Vonsha Blow, who died on the basketball court during Woodham High School's summer program in 1998. Thank you.

Thanks to Dan Shugart and WEAR Channel 3 news for covering me in my high school years of playing basketball, coaching high school basketball, and my years training boxers.

Special thanks to Derrick Brooks, who always believed in my talent as a trainer and also invited me to one of his Tampa Bay Buccaneers games.

Much love to Fred Robbins, Super Bowl champion with the New York Giants. He represents my home neighborhood of Lincoln Park. He was good enough to give me a game jersey when he played with the Minnesota Vikings.

Thanks to County Commissioner Luman May who always answered my phone calls and helped me with the Evander Holyfield Boxing Camp.

I want to give a shout-out to Linda "Sunshine" Moore at the WRRX-FM 106.1 morning show for holding it down for Pensacola for twenty-six years.

RIP to Tupac Shakur who I had a chance to chill with in Atlanta, GA. He was a real cool brother. He gave me his phone number and signature and invited me to give him a call when Roy and I come to Vegas, so we could hang out. Gone too soon!

Folks say I look like Cedric the Entertainer and even act like him. We've gotta be distant cousins or something. I'm glad I had a chance to meet him. His was the first comedy show I promoted in Pensacola. Later on, we got to hang in Atlantic City together, walking the boardwalk and joking around all day. I'm proud of the life he lives making people laugh, and I try to do the same.

At a Jordan celebrity golf tournament in the Bahamas, I had the chance to dance with Gabrielle Union, and I couldn't believe how down-to-earth she was. When I told her that, she laughed and said, "Man, I'm from Omaha, Nebraska." (Of course, I told my wife about the dance.)

I regret not taking up an invitation to go eat dinner with Joe Jackson because I felt like he was going to get mad at me for asking for Janet Jackson's phone number.

Shout out to Ice Cube, who I had the chance to meet. Jokingly I told Ice Cube that Roy had a fight coming up and asked if would he come to Pensacola and spar Roy. Ice Cube said, "Who me, spar Roy? HELL NO."

I said, "But you beat Deebo!" Ice Cube looked at me crazy and said, "N****r, dats the movie."

Shout out to the Flight Gang DraE featuring gLeNn. Coming up as young boys DraE and gLeNn were always close to me. It was an honor to coach them during their twelfth-grade year of high school basketball. Now they are adults, and they are still remarkably close to me. I am proud of the two boys for having their song "Hoop Dreams" chosen to be on "NBA 2K21." Not only that, but they selected me as their manager.

I got a chance to see one of my wife's favorite singers perform up close, Mary J. Blige. Mary J. was gracious enough to offer to autograph the picture we took together. Mary, I'm still waiting for your address.

Shout out to legendary quarterback Randall Cunningham, who I had the pleasure to meet.

Shout out to Shaquille O'Neal who I got to talk to a little bit and just missed the chance to hang out with while he was with Magic.

To my brother, Faizon Love, who is kind enough to help support me in promoting this book and is one of the realest brothers I know.

I wanna holla at Adrian Chambers who played for the Cardinals and won a World Series and to Reggie Evans (aka "Joker") one of the hardest rebounders to ever play the game.

To New Orleans Saints Super Bowl Champ Coach Sean Payton, who was gracious enough to get me and Roy tickets to a game. Roy gave a speech to pump up the team, so we feel like we shared a piece of their Super Bowl win later that year. So Coach, we're still waiting on our Super Bowl rings!

Shamar Moore did not believe I watched The Young & the Restless every day. I called Roy over where we were standing. I asked him, "What do I always ask the housekeeping ladies to help me find on the TV?" Roy replied without hesitation, "The Young and the Restless," and started laughing.

After one of Jalen Rose's games, we were introduced to each other and we immediately hit it off and became friends. We exchanged phone numbers and would chat from time to time.

Shout out to my brother-in-law Eddie Johnson (aka TJ). It's been a lot of good times we've had together, and I'm proud to call you my brother. I still remember when you called me in tears after listening to I'm Coming Home by New Edition thinking about Fee Fee.

Many thanks to J.J. Tolbert and his law firm who

helped me put on my first boxing camp with Evander Holyfield.

If you just so happen to stop by the gym when Roy Jones and I are training, the music playlist you'll hear includes the Body Head Bangers, Ice Cube, Snoop Dogg, Run DMC, Mystikal, Rick Ross, Mobb Deep, and of course, Scarface. I would love to give a shout-out to James Prince (aka Lil' Jay) and the entire Rap-A-Lot family.

Shout-out to my homeboys who were on "Pros vs. Joes," where I became good friends with Hall of Fame running back Eric Dickerson, baseball Hall of Famer Vince Coleman, "Mr. Crossover" Tim Hardaway, Bruce Smith, and Kevin Willis.

One more shout out to the boys from New Edition. I love your music so much. That's why I'm gonna hate to have to beat Mike and Ronnie in a three-point shooting contest against me and Roy. I'll even spot you ten!

I'm proud of the men I've been privileged to train in the ring and honored to share a few quotes from them about our friendships.

Alfred "Ice" Cole: He got a lot of experience and knowledge working with so many top fighters—but also other top fighters that came from Pensacola, FL like Derrick Smoke Gainer and Billy Lewis as another top ten fighters in the world.

Jason Papillion: Where do I start? I met Alfy Smith—"Big Al"—in 1990. I remember him picking me up from the bus station in his Jeep with the music blasting. This is a relationship that still stands firm after twenty-plus years. It started off with him picking me up every day from the hotel and bringing me to the boxing gym to becoming my head trainer and brother.

After most of the training sessions, he would bring me over to his house, and that is where I had the great pleasure of meeting my second family. I met his late mother, Elizabeth, and his late brother, Vonsha, and they made me feel like I was at home.

Then he took me to meet his family; two daughters, Jada Boo and Kia, who I literally watched grow up into beautiful young ladies, and his beautiful wife, the late Felicia "Fee Fee" Smith. There is so much I can say about her. She was the humblest person I know. She took to me like I was her son. From that time, staying at the hotel was over. She told me to come and stay at their home. She did it all as if I was her son. She washed my clothes, cooked my food, and did my shopping. She did it all. I still remember the time Fee Fee and Big Al showed up for my surprise birthday party. I turned around and seen those two and bust out crying tears of joy, a night I will always cherish.

The Smiths got a chance to meet my family in 1999 for my fight in Lafayette, Louisiana, and we all became one big family. With Big Al as my trainer, we traveled the world together, and we won the NABF Jr Middleweight Title together.

I will never forget the night Fee Fee passed. Me and my family had just left from visiting them at their home in Pensacola. Fee Fee hugged me extra tight when we were leaving to come back home (I guess it was her way of telling me goodbye), and my wife told her, "We'll see y'all for vacation."

Fee didn't answer back like she would normally do.

When we got back to Lafayette, I went on Facebook to tell my friends that we had arrived safely, and I saw a post from Alfy's daughter, Jada. She wrote that she had almost lost her mom. I called Alfy right away. He told me that Fee Fee was gone. I bust out hollering and yelling in grief. My wife kept asking, "What's wrong? What's wrong?" but I couldn't catch my breath enough to tell her.

One of the hardest rides I ever had was driving back to Pensacola to put my second mom to rest.

Mark Lanton: Alfy Smith is more than a world-class trainer or coach. He is a great friend that brought out the best in a boxer. He understood me as an individual, and his unique approach brought out the best boxer in me. I was blessed to have Alfy literally in my corner.

Victor "Mista" Mckinnis: About Alfy the Trainer and friend, I met Alfy back in the mid-nineties at the Square Ring Boxing Gym in Pensacola. He was a friend of Roy Jones, Jr and thus became a friend of the gym. I saw Alfy come from being a former basketball player to a boxing trainer. He was always willing to learn and even take a few body blows, (very few, lol!).

Alfy moved from beginner to true technician. He was then and is now an even better man and personifies the very definition of friend. The brother is just cool, and I do not mean riding in a car or dating a lot of women. I mean cool as in peaceful to be around, so you feel cool as well. Alfy is truly all that and a bag of chips. (Look at his waist, Lol!) I am grateful to know this man as a former athlete, trainer, coach, and most of all friend.

I want to close these acknowledgements the way I started, with Roy Jones Jr. I offer my own brotherly words of love to Roy, without whom I might not have had the chance to write this book. I made Roy a promise that we would start together on top and end together on top, and that is what true dedication is about.

CPSIA information can be obtained
at www.ICGtesting.com
Printed in the USA
BVHW090835210922
647550BV00006B/104